The Testimony of Jesus—is the Spirit of Prophecy

School of the Holy Spirit
Manual 3a

Thierry Nakoa

Supernatural Lifestyle Manual Series

SCHOOLOFTHEHOLYSPIRIT.CHURCH

Published by Thierry Nakoa

KJV
Unless otherwise noted, all scriptures are from the KING JAMES VERSION (KJV): KING JAMES VERSION, public domain.

NKJV
Scripture taken from the New King James Version®. Copyright © 1982 by Thomas Nelson. Used by permission. All rights reserved.
Several Scripture quotations include the author's emphasis; the added emphasis is shown in italic/underlined/bolded text. Printed in the United States of America

ISBN: 978-1-963465-03-7 *Paperback*
ISBN: 978-1-963465-00-6 *E-Book*
ISBN: 978-1-963465-13-6 *Paperback Spanish*

© SCHOOL OF THE HOLY SPIRIT

P.O. Box 1197
Irmo, SC
29063-2867 United States

DEDICATION

This manual is dedicated to my wife and son, both of whom selflessly sacrificed their time so that I could devote myself to serving others. I would also like to extend my dedication to my apostolic leaders, Danny and Karen Steyne, who are genuine leaders in the faith.

Contents

Blank Page

ACKNOWLEDGMENTS

I would like to express my gratitude to all my colleagues in the School of the Holy Spirit who provided me with enthusiastic support and encouragement in the creation of this training manual. Especially to those who consistently showed up to support me and to those who helped with the edits and development of the activations, I am truly grateful. For over 25 years, I have been fortunate to have fathers and mothers in my life who laid down the essential groundwork for the prophetic. Their influence has allowed me to be present in this moment, passing on revelation to the next generation, and for that, I am truly thankful.

Prophecy

What is Prophecy?

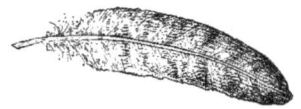

And though I have _the gift of prophecy_, and _understand_ all _mysteries_, and all _knowledge_...
—1 Corinthians 13:2a

And I fell at his feet to worship him. And he said unto me, see thou do it not: I am thy fellow servant, and of thy brethren that have the testimony of Jesus: worship God: _for the testimony of Jesus is the spirit of prophecy._
—Revelation 19:10

"The Testimony of Jesus is the Spirit of Prophecy"

The Greek word for prophecy is prophēteuō. Προφητεύω|prophēteuō

Thayer's Definition: _to prophesy, to be a prophet, speak forth by divine inspirations, to predict._

- _with the idea of foretelling future events pertaining especially to the kingdom of God_
- _to utter forth, declare, a thing which can only be known by divine revelation_
- _to break forth under sudden impulse in lofty discourse or praise of the divine counsels_
- _under like prompting, to teach, refute, reprove, admonish, comfort others_
- _to act as a prophet, discharge the prophetic office_[1]

Biblical prophecy can serve the purpose of _foretelling_ or _forth telling_, which involves the ability to see into the future or _creatively_ speak things into existence. In addition, prophecies can _unveil mysteries_, offering divine comprehension, insight, and revelation that surpass individual concerns. Prophecies can provide oversight by granting supernatural _knowledge_ of nations, states, and even knowing the presence of evil territorial spirits.

---

[1] Joseph Thayer, ed., _Thayer's Greek-English Lexicon of the New Testament: Coded with Strong's Concordance Numbers_, Reissue,Subsequent edition (Massachusetts: Hendrickson Academic, 1995).

Finally, prophecies can provide knowledge and insight, both on a personal level and for the benefit of communities, nations, and an *understanding* of times and seasons. Speaking the mind of God to encourage and build up the church.

A PROPHECY CAN ENCOMPASS:

1. Foretell (foresight; *see the future ahead, or* 'to show His [Jesus'] servants—things which must shortly take place." Revelation 1:1b).

2. Forth tell (creative; "calling those things which be not as though they were." Romans 4:17b 1 Kings 17:1).

3. Revealing Mysteries 1 Corinthians 13:2a (Oversight; *divine understanding, wisdom and revelation-not only personal, supernatural knowledge of/for nations and states, territories*).

4. Understanding Knowledge 1 Corinthians 13:2a (Insight; *personal and for communities or nations, times, and seasons.* Speaking the mind of God to encourage and build up the church, reading the mind and spirit of man).

   And Samuel answered Saul, and said, I am the seer: go up before me unto the high place; for ye shall eat with me today, and tomorrow I will let thee go, and will tell thee all that is in thine heart. —1 Samuel 9:19 And one of his servants said, None, my lord, O king: but Elisha, the prophet that is in Israel, telleth the king of Israel the words that thou speakest in thy bed chamber. —2 Kings 6:12

5. According to the Midrash, prophecy encompasses not just prediction and fulfillment, but also biblical patterns. The principle of "expositional constancy" serves as a prime example of the patterned nature of biblical prophecy. Additional examples may be discovered via typological and foreshadowing methods.

PERSONAL PROPHECY

Personal prophecy is for the benefit of another. *Prophecy should bring people closer to loving Jesus.* This should be the litmus test for testing and judging the prophetic. True prophetic words, whether it is for a nation or an individual, should promote Jesus Christ and His Kingdom. Although the gift of tongues is the entrance to the gifts of the Holy Spirit, the gift of prophecy is the one which transcends and crosses the border into the other categories.

TO SPEAK ON BEHALF OF GOD

But the LORD said unto me, say not, I am a child: for thou shalt go to all that I shall send thee, and whatsoever I command thee thou shalt speak. —Jeremiah 1:7

The Lord commanded the Prophets to speak and repeat His very words to the people of Israel. It didn't matter if you were a youth or underprivileged.

THE TESTIMONY OF JESUS IS THE SPIRIT OF PROPHECY

The Spirit of Prophecy is the testimony of Jesus, and vice versa. The verse in Revelation 19:10c is a major key to understanding the prophetic. It reveals that Jesus is the centerpiece as it relates to learning how prophecy works. *The Spirit of Jesus* is the Spirit of Prophecy. Jesus is the Word of God. Jesus is God. God is not bound by any space nor time. As a matter of truth, everything was created in Him, for Him, by Him before the boundary of space, time, or matter existed. Jesus is the substance of everything that exist invisible or visible. If Jesus or His Spirit was bound by time then He is not God. Jesus created time and space for His creation and His heavens and earth purposes. Time to humans is a jail cell in terms of eternity. Only but a vapor. Jesus or His Spirit—the Spirit of prophecy—are eternal and everlasting. He Who is, Who was, and Will ever be doesn't need anything. Hence, He is the, I am that I am (YHVH). The Spirit of Prophecy is anchored on Jesus. It is not anchored on the earth or the heavens. This is why the Bible says, Jesus was slain before the foundations of the earth.

"In the beginning" is not a time in space, but it is a location in God Himself...(specifically the Hebraic alphabet or alefbet called the *bet*— represents Christ). God precedes time. He most definitely precedes "times and seasons" which He established during creation.

David in his famous quote sees and hear this:

> *The LORD hath sworn, and will not repent,*
> *Thou art a priest for ever after the order of Melchizedek. —Psalms 110:4*

This occurred in the heaven of the heavens and outside of our time and space constraints.

So now the fulfillment is according to His will and timing (not our times and seasons) He says:

> *The LORD said unto my Lord,*
> *Sit thou at my right hand,*
> <u>*until*</u> *I make thine enemies thy footstool. —Psalms 110:1*

The word the Father used was "until" I make your enemies your footstool. Very common for God to use a "marker" word prophecy.

God's omniscience goes beyond the boundaries of time; He not only sees us in the present but also in the past and future. Moreover, His knowledge of us is not limited to mere observation, as He has predestined us even before the inception of time. Not only does He have knowledge of us in the present, but He also foreknows us after time and into eternity. The writer of the book of Hebrews briefly mentions that "*the power of the age to come*" has the remarkable ability to transcend time and space, and it is reserved for those who have reached a level of maturity, rather than those who are still considered infants.

God is sovereign and He can speak the way He wants to.

> *The secret of the LORD is with them that fear Him;*
> *and he will shew them his covenant. —Psalms 25:14*

GOD'S SECRETS

According to this scripture, those who fear the Lord or walk in "the spirit of the fear of the Lord" have the privilege of knowing the secrets or the hidden mysteries of God.

> Surely the Lord GOD will do nothing,
> but He revealeth His secret unto His servants the prophets.
> The lion hath roared, who will not fear?
> the Lord GOD hath spoken, who can but prophesy? —Amos 3:7-8

SIGNS OF THE LAST DAYS OUTPOURING IS THE PROPHETIC ANOINTING

Jesus' servants, specifically the prophets, are among those who fear the Lord. The utterances of the Lord to His servants bear the resemblance of a lion's mighty roar, and the recipients can only respond by echoing a word of prophecy. The weight of the Lord's burden is so formidable that one can only prophesy after experiencing such a resounding sound. The ground trembles as anything capable of shaking is shaken.

> Yet the LORD testified against Israel, and against Judah, by all the prophets, and by all the seers, saying, Turn ye from your evil ways, and keep my commandments and my statutes, according to all the law which I commanded your fathers, and which I sent to you by my servants the prophets. —2 Kings 17:13

> But in the days of the voice of the seventh angel, when he shall begin to sound, the mystery of God should be finished, as he hath declared to _His servants the prophets._ —Revelation 10:7

> God, who at sundry times and _in divers manners spake in time past unto the fathers by the prophets,_ Hath in these last days spoken unto us by _His Son,_ whom he hath appointed heir of all things, by whom also he made the worlds; —Hebrews 1:1-2

> And he said unto me, these sayings are faithful and true: and the Lord God of _the holy prophets_ sent his angel to shew unto _His servants the things which must shortly be done._ —Revelation 22:6

In the history of Israel and Judah, the Lord dispatched prophets as His servants to deliver correction, warning, and judgments. The prophets in times past mainly sent a message of repentance to the wayward people of God. God's mysteries were revealed by the prophets and personified in Jesus. The prophets were called to be holy in order to carry the message of the coming of the Lord. The Fear of the Lord is holiness. Holiness empowers the transmission of God's unadulterated word to the people. Through the use of prophecy, the Lord is able to effectively communicate His intentions and will. This divine communication is carried out by the saints who fear Him and His faithful servants, known as the prophets.

> For _ye may all prophesy_ one by one, that all may learn, and all may be comforted. —1 Corinthians 14

> "You may all prophesy"

And it shall come to pass in the last days, saith God, <u>I will pour out of my Spirit upon all flesh</u>: and your sons and your daughters <u>shall prophesy</u>, and your young men shall see visions, and your old men shall dream dreams: —Acts 2:17

Today, the Lord has poured out His Spirit on all flesh and all will prophesy about the goodness of God. Hearing God's voice is not only reserved for prophets but also for those who are obedient and have the fear of the Lord. Believing that God speaks to us is the first step to intentionally hearing from Him. The prophetic journey begins by recognizing that God still speaks and we can listen to His voice.

Reflections, Reviews, Questions

1. What is the testimony of Jesus?

_____

_____

_____

_____

2. As a believer of Jesus Christ, do you believe you possess the ability to prophesy?

_____

_____

_____

_____

Notes

_____

_____

_____

_____

_____

_____

_____

_____

_____

_____

_____

_____

_____

_____

Prophetic Levels of Responsibility

LEVELS OF PROPHETIC RESPONSIBILITY

For <u>ye may all prophesy</u> one by one, that all may learn, and all may be comforted.
—1 Corinthians 14:31

All individuals possess the capacity to provide comfort, edification, and exhortation to others. When beginning to prophesy, everyone should start here.

The Spirit of Prophecy (the entire pool of water is the testimony of Jesus)

| Untrained **Called** | Trained **Training** | Officed **Commissioned** |

Occasionally prophetic

Regularly Prophetic

Spirit of Prophecy (Rev 19:10c, 1 Cor 14:31, Act 2:17)

Comfort
Edification (building)
Exhortation (encouraging)
the entire pool

The shallow end of the pool: **Saints** or the Priesthood of every believer. *But ye are a chosen generation, a royal priesthood, a holy nation, a peculiar people;*
—1 Peter 2:9a

The Gift of Prophecy 1 Cor 13:2a

"though I have *the gift of prophecy*, and understand all *mysteries* and all *knowledge*"

The Middle of pool
Gifted Saints or
Gifted Priests
To another prophecy...
—1 Corinthians 12:10b

The Prophethood Eph 4:11

Calling Stage (0–5yrs)
Training Stage (15–25yrs)
Office Stage (training never ends. Glory to Glory)

The Deep end of pool
Prophets
"And he gave some, apostles; and some, <u>prophets</u>; and some, evangelists; and some, pastors and teachers;"
—Ephesians 4:11

FIGURE 1 PROPHETIC LEVELS OF RESPONSIBILITY

The Prophethood

THE CALLING STAGE

The Lord Calls Samuel

And the child Samuel ministered unto the LORD before Eli. And the word of the LORD was precious in those days; there was no open vision. And it came to pass at that time, when Eli was laid down in his place, and his eyes began to wax dim, that he could not see; And ere the lamp of God went out in the temple of the LORD, where the ark of God was, and Samuel was laid down to sleep; That the LORD called Samuel: and he answered, Here am I. And he ran unto Eli, and said, Here am I; for thou calledst me. And he said, I called not; lie down again. And he went and lay down. And the LORD called yet again, Samuel. And Samuel arose and went to Eli, and said, Here am I; for thou didst call me. And he answered, I called not, my son; lie down again. Now Samuel did not yet know the LORD, neither was the word of the LORD yet revealed unto him. And the LORD called Samuel again the third time. And he arose and went to Eli, and said, Here am I; for thou didst call me. And Eli perceived that the LORD had called the child. Therefore Eli said unto Samuel, Go, lie down: and it shall be, if he call thee, that thou shalt say, Speak, LORD; for thy servant heareth. So Samuel went and lay down in his place. And the LORD came, and stood, and called as at other times, Samuel, Samuel. Then Samuel answered, Speak; for thy servant heareth. And the LORD said to Samuel, Behold, I will do a thing in Israel, at which both the ears of every one that heareth it shall tingle. In that day I will perform against Eli all things which I have spoken concerning his house: when I begin, I will also make an end. For I have told him that I will judge his house for ever for the iniquity which he knoweth; because his sons made themselves vile, and he restrained them not. And therefore I have sworn unto the house of Eli, that the iniquity of Eli's house shall not be purged with sacrifice nor offering for ever. And Samuel lay until the morning, and opened the doors of the house of the LORD. And Samuel feared to shew Eli the vision. Then Eli called Samuel, and said, Samuel, my son. And he answered, Here am I. And he said, What is the thing that the LORD hath said unto thee? I pray thee hide it not from me: God do so to thee, and more also, if thou hide any thing from me of all the things that he said unto thee. And Samuel told him every whit, and hid nothing from him. And he said, It is the LORD: let him do what seemeth him good.—1 Samuel 3:1-18

Similar to Samuel's calling, many individuals are called to serve, but only a handful progress to the office stage. It can be compared to a woman's pregnancy phase prior to giving birth. In the calling stage, the initial confirmations of the office call are being declared. During this stage of calling, you have the opportunity to explore and uncover your purpose as well as the various tasks that await you.

And he gave some, apostles; and some, prophets; and some, evangelists; and some, pastors and teachers; For the perfecting of the saints, for the work of the ministry, for the edifying of the body of Christ: Till we all come in the unity of the faith, and of the knowledge of the Son of God, unto a perfect man, unto the measure of the stature of the fulness of Christ: —Ephesians 4:11-13

For many are called, but few are chosen. —Matthew 22:14

Jesus Himself gave gifts unto men as gifts to the Church to train the saints. The calling of many people is comparable to that of a pregnant woman in an embryonic stage. Therefore, if complications arise before birth, it is possible that the baby will not reach full term. Many are called, but few will pass their process and testing to get to their office stage.

THE TRAINED/TRAINING STAGE:

And the child Samuel grew on, and was in favour both with the LORD, and also with men. —1 Samuel 2:26

This charge I commit unto thee, son Timothy, according to the prophecies which went before on thee, that thou by them mightest war a good warfare; —1 Timothy 1:18

Neither went I up to Jerusalem to them which were apostles before me; but I went into Arabia, and returned again unto Damascus. Then after three years I went up to Jerusalem to see Peter, and abode with him fifteen days. —Galatians 1:17-18

I knew a man in Christ above <u>fourteen years ago</u>, (whether in the body, I cannot tell; or whether out of the body, I cannot tell: God knoweth;) such an one caught up to the third heaven. —2 Corinthians 12:2

Then <u>fourteen years after</u> I went up again to Jerusalem with Barnabas, and took Titus with me also. And I went up by revelation, and communicated unto them that gospel which I preach among the Gentiles, but privately to them which were of reputation, lest by any means I should run, or had run, in vain. —Galatians 2:1-2

THE COMMISSIONED/OFFICE STAGE:

And Samuel grew, and the LORD was with him, and did let none of his words fall to the ground. And <u>all Israel from Dan even to Beersheba knew that Samuel was established to be a prophet of the LORD</u>. And the LORD appeared again in Shiloh: for <u>the LORD revealed himself to Samuel</u> in Shiloh by the word of the LORD. —1 Samuel 3:19-21

It took Samuel 25 years to be recognized as an established prophet, starting from when Eli taught him to hear the voice of the Lord. It took Jeremiah approximately 17 years to be commissioned as an established prophet. It was after 40 years for Moses to get commissioned into his position as a prophet, priest, and king (a King-Priest, or a Melchizedek, refer to School of the Holy Spirit Manual number 8— Royal Priesthood).

THE DOMA GIFTS VS THE CHARISMA GIFTS

Δομα | doma |

The Greek word "Doma" can be found in four instances in the KJV, namely Matthew 7:11, Luke 11:13, Ephesians 4:8, and Philippians 4:17, as mentioned in Mounce's Expository Greek Dictionary[2]. The meaning of this word can be summed up as a simple gift or present. According to Larry Randolph, there is a distinction between the Charisma gift mentioned in Corinthians and the Doma Gift, as the latter possesses governmental influence and position. It should be noted that these gifts are different from the Charisma ones and possess their own individual characteristics. On certain occasions, we come across numerous individuals who possess the remarkable gift of Prophecy and Charisma, but when they attempt to exercise their abilities within the office setting, complications arise. The ascension gifts mentioned in Ephesians 4:11 from Jesus Himself come with different kinds of responsibilities and authority, resulting in a certain level of influence. Our Lord Jesus has outlined that the ascension or Doma gifts are meant to be used for the purpose of building and perfecting the saints until the Bride is completely spotless and without wrinkles. These authoritative gifts fulfill the "Pleroma" (the mending of the nets) the fullness of time in our dispensation toward the work of the kingdom of occupying till Jesus' eminent return. In fact, they are building architectural foundations to make the bride ready for the Lord. These gifts signify more than just influence and authority; they bring power and unity, transforming nations and cultures to abide in the fear of the Lord. They cause chiropractic shifts in the body, leading to transformations and revolutions in past practices.

A PROPHECY IS PART OF THE WHOLE.

For we know in part, and we prophesy in part. —1 Corinthians 13:9

To those who fear Him and His prophets, the Lord unveils His secrets. Connecting the released prophetic word to other prophetic words is necessary for understanding the big picture. No individual, besides Jesus, can comprehend the complete prophetic word they deliver. The fulfillment of certain prophetic words can span significant periods of time, including decades, centuries, millenniums, and even ages. In order to comprehend prophecies, one must adopt the viewpoint of God, who exists beyond the limitations of time and space. To truly comprehend the entire picture, we must acknowledge that Jesus is the key to its fulfillment, both at the cross and in His second coming. Therefore, it is important for us to understand the perspectives of end-time eschatology properly.

The prophet's ability to prophesy is influenced by the prophetic flow or anointing, and they can also perceive when someone else is about to prophesy. Additionally, this also indicates that the prophet has the ability to commence their prophesying and conclude it at their own discretion.

---

[2] William D. Mounce, *Mounce's Complete Expository Dictionary of Old and New Testament Words*, Supersaver ed. edition (Grand Rapids (Mich.): Zondervan Academic, 2006).

Reflections, Reviews, Questions

3. What distinguishes the Saints, the gifted Saints, and the called Prophets?

_____

_____

4. Do you think that the gift of prophecy is limited only to personal prophecy?

_____

_____

5. Explain The Prophetic Levels of Responsibility (refer to Figure 1):

_____

_____

_____

Notes

_____

_____

_____

_____

_____

_____

_____

_____

_____

The differences between the Gift of Prophecy and the Office of a Prophet

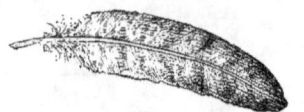

The differences between the Gift of prophecy and the office of a prophet	
The Gift of Prophecy (some with the gift) as Gift from the Holy Spirit. 1 Corinthians 12:10; 14 (Fully matured or trained gift)	The Office (some prophets) Gift from Jesus Christ. Ephesian 4:11 (Fully matured or trained and mentored into the office)
Comforting, Edifying, Exhortation Those in leadership have the responsibility to direct, correct, and warn those under their authority. **Some with the gift (Charisma).** *And though I have the gift of prophecy, and <u>understand all mysteries, and all knowledge,</u>... I am nothing.* —1 Corinthians 13:2a Those who have the gift or eldership can impart it via the laying on of hands and prophecy. *Neglect not the gift that is in thee, which was <u>given thee by prophecy,</u> with the <u>laying on of the hands</u> of the presbytery.* —1 Timothy 4:14	Comfort, Edify, Exhort plus **Direction, Correction, Warning** The **person is the Gift** to the Church and operates in the Gift of Prophecy as well. *And he gave some, apostles; and some, prophets; and some, evangelists; and some, pastors and teachers; For the perfecting of the saints, for the work of the ministry, for the edifying of the body of Christ: Till we all come in the unity of the faith, and of the knowledge of the Son of God, unto a perfect man, unto the measure of the stature of the fulness of Christ:* —Ephesians 4:11-13 Some are the gift in the Church (Doma) *Are all apostles? are <u>all prophets?</u> are all teachers? are all workers of miracles? Have all the gifts of healing? do all speak with tongues? do all interpret? But covet earnestly the best gifts: and yet shew I unto you a more excellent way.* —1 Corinthians 12:29-31
GIFT OF PROPHECY	OFFICE OF A PROPHET

The differences between the Gift of prophecy and the office of a prophet	
Needs Training to develop skills.	**Needs Training to develop skills.**
As they receive training and are equipped, they develop a greater level of acuteness and refinement. Prophetic Teaching/Preaching capable via the gift of prophecy by revealing mysteries and knowledge. **The gift cannot be purchased.** *And when Simon saw that through laying on of the apostles' hands the Holy Ghost was given, he offered them money, Saying, Give me also this power, that on whomsoever I lay hands, he may receive the Holy Ghost. But Peter said unto him, <u>Thy money perish with thee, because thou hast thought that the gift of God may be purchased with money.</u> Thou hast neither part nor lot in this matter: for thy heart is not right in the sight of God.* *—Acts 8:18-21* **You can receive it via the preaching of the Word.** *While Peter yet spake these words, <u>the Holy Ghost fell on all them which heard the word.</u> And they of the circumcision which believed were astonished, as many as came with Peter, because that on the Gentiles also was poured out the gift of the Holy Ghost. For they heard <u>them speak with tongues, and magnify God.</u> Then answered Peter, —Acts 10:44-4*	Can impart gifts by prophecy with the laying on of the hands of the eldership. —1 Timothy 4:14 *And the spirits of the prophets are <u>subject to the prophets.</u> —1 Corinthians 14:32* The prophet's ability to prophesy is influenced by the prophetic flow or anointing, and they can also perceive when someone else is about to prophesy. Additionally, this also indicates that the prophet has the ability to commence their prophesying and conclude it at their own discretion. **The office cannot be purchased nor imparted to** God alone determines who is born as a prophet and called. Your call to serve comes directly from Jesus Himself, not from men. Impartation cannot transform someone into a prophet if they are not called to be one. Prophets not only do personal prophecies, but they are involved in building foundational truths which matures the body of Christ. They are instrumental in the overall structure and operation of the Church as a whole within their jurisdiction or scope of influence. They are not merely preoccupied with building one person, but the collective. This is why they are not only people with gifts operating in the Body, but they are the instruments that catalyzes the church into forward motion.
GIFT OF PROPHECY	OFFICE OF A PROPHET

The differences between the Gift of prophecy and the office of a prophet	
GIFT OF PROPHECY	OFFICE OF A PROPHET
	From whom the whole body fitly joined together and compacted by that which every joint supplieth, according to the effectual working in the measure of every part, **maketh increase of the body** *unto the edifying of itself in love.* —Ephesians 4:16d Their lives embody the word or lifetime message, the prophet is also the message to a nation or a time or age. **_And the Word was made flesh,_** _and dwelt among us_—John 1:14a The stage or phase of the Prophethood and Metron cycle determines the governmental authority of prophets. This authority can extend to various levels, such as the church, community, region, country, or even nations. **Forth telling** *(requires more anointing for this)* *Has more creative force or might in the prophetic— To call things out as though they were. (By my word there shall be nor due or rain).* —1 Kings 17:1 *Speaking those things as though they were. Partnering with the Father and what He is doing.*
GIFT OF PROPHECY	OFFICE OF A PROPHET

The differences between the Gift of prophecy and the office of a prophet	
GIFT OF PROPHECY	**OFFICE OF A PROPHET**
	Equips and Trains the People *Catalysts, Activates, Impart, Initiators, and Establishes, Builds and Trains, Multiplies Himself, Creates Prophetic Cultures, Releases, Call others into their destinies* **Architect and Chiropractor of the Body (builders)** *Establishes Church foundational Doctrines alongside the apostles* *having been* **built** *on* **the foundation of the apostles and prophets**, *Jesus Christ Himself being the chief cornerstone,* —Eph 2:20 NKJV *And are* **built** *upon* **the foundation of the apostles and prophets**, *Jesus Christ himself being the chief corner stone;* —Ephesians 2:20 **Leads the Church alongside apostles.** Speaks judgment and grace on behalf of God Prophetic Teaching/Preaching capable via the gift of prophecy by revealing mysteries and knowledge **Needs Training to develop skills**
GIFT OF PROPHECY	**OFFICE OF A PROPHET**

ALL BELIEVERS CAN PROPHESY

For ye may all prophesy one by one, that all may learn, and all may be comforted. —1 Corinthians 14:31

*And **though I have the gift of prophecy**, and understand all **mysteries**, and all **knowledge**; and though I have all faith, so that I could remove mountains, and have not charity, I am nothing.* —1 Corinthians 13:2a

*Neglect not **the gift that is in thee**, which was given thee by prophecy, with the laying on of the hands of the presbytery.* —1 Timothy 4:14

In 1 Timothy 4:14, it is clearly stated that one can disregard the gifts that have been bestowed upon them through the act of the presbytery—laying on of hands. We must actively seek and participate in using our gifts, whether it's prophecy or other gifts.

And Moses said unto him, Enviest thou for my sake? would God that all the LORD'S people were prophets, and that the LORD would put his spirit upon them! —Numbers 11:29

It is the desire of the Lord to place His Spirit upon His people. This means that He desire all His people to be a prophetic people. Because when we saw the spirit of Moses which was in fact the Spirit of the Lord or the Spirit of Jesus is the spirit of Prophecy.

The Lord desires to place His Spirit upon His people. This signifies that His intention is for each and every one of His people to have the ability to prophesy. The spirit of Moses, also known as the Spirit of the Lord or the Spirit of Jesus, is intrinsically linked to the spirit of Prophecy.

HEARING THE VOICE OF GOD OR ACTIVATING SPIRITUAL SENSES

*For the LORD has poured out on you The spirit of deep sleep, And has closed your eyes, namely, **the prophets**; And He has covered your heads, namely, **the seers**.* —Isaiah 29:10 NKJV

*For the LORD hath poured out upon you the spirit of deep sleep, and hath closed your eyes: **the prophets** and your rulers, **the seers** hath he covered.* —Isaiah 29:10 KJV

HEARING

My sheep hear my voice, and I know them, and they follow me: —*John 10:27*

Therefore Eli said unto Samuel, Go, lie down: and it shall be, if he call thee, that thou shalt say, Speak, LORD; for thy servant heareth. So Samuel went and lay down in his place. —*1 Samuel 3:9*

SEEING

I counsel thee to buy of me gold tried in the fire, that thou mayest be rich; and white raiment, that thou mayest be clothed, and that the shame of thy nakedness do not appear; and anoint thine eyes with eyesalve, that thou mayest see. —*Revelation 3:18*

I will stand upon my watch, and set me upon the tower, and will watch to see what he will say unto me, and what I shall answer when I am reproved. And the LORD answered me, and said, Write the vision, and make it plain upon tables, that he may run that readeth it. For the vision is yet for an appointed time, but at the end it shall speak, and not lie: though it tarry, wait for it; because it will surely come, it will not tarry. Behold, his soul which is lifted up is not upright in him: but the just shall live by his faith. —*Habakkuk 2:1-4*

(For we walk by faith, not by **sight***:)* — *2 Corinthians 5:7*

According to Strong Concordance, The Greek word for the Sight is εἶδος | **eidos: a** form, external appearance. Luke 3:22 and John 5:37 both contain references to the mentioned shape. Luke 9:29 is translated as "Fashion," whereas in 1 Thessalonians 5:22, it can be translated as "Kind," "species," or "appearance." The translation of "sight" or "perception" is seen in 2 Corinthians 5:7.

In 2 Corinthians 5:7, the word "sight" is used to denote our five physical senses. If we replace "sight" with "five senses", the bigger picture becomes clear. "For we walk by faith, not by [*our five senses*]." — 2Co 5:7 Let's emulate Jesus as described in Isaiah 11:3 which says "His delight is in the fear of the LORD, And He shall <u>not judge by the sight of His eyes, nor decide by the hearing of His ears.</u> Jesus exercised judgment through the operation of the Spirit of the fear of the Lord, which bestowed upon Him supernatural knowledge.

If I have told you <u>earthly things</u>, and ye believe not, how shall ye believe, if I tell you of <u>heavenly things?</u> —*John 3:12*

To emulate Jesus' approach of explaining spiritual concepts, we must adequately address their manifestations in the natural or earthly realm. We are not saying that there are five spiritual senses per se, but we can use the five natural senses to confirm the spiritual senses in the spirit that are similarly equivalent. To gain a comprehensive understanding of the spiritual senses, it is crucial to comprehend their functioning within the invisible realm or the spiritual world. The story of the rich man and Lazarus, found in Luke 16:19-31, provides us with a clear example of how we can see this concept in action.

> There was a certain rich man, which was clothed in purple and fine linen, and fared sumptuously every day: —20 And there was **a certain beggar named Lazarus**, which was laid at his gate, full of sores, —21 And desiring to be fed with the crumbs which fell from the rich man's table: moreover the dogs came and licked his sores. —22 And it came to pass, that the beggar died, and was carried by the angels into Abraham's bosom: the **rich man also died**, and was buried; —23 And in hell he lift up his eyes, being in torments, and **seeth** Abraham afar off, and Lazarus in his bosom. —24 And **he cried and said**, Father Abraham, have mercy on me, and send Lazarus, that **he may dip the tip of his finger in water, and cool my tongue**; for I am **tormented in this flame**. —25 But Abraham said, Son, remember that thou in thy lifetime receivedst thy good things, and likewise Lazarus evil things: but now he is comforted, and thou art tormented. —26 And beside all this, between us and you there is a great gulf fixed: so that they which would pass from hence to you cannot; neither can they pass to us, that would come from thence. —27 Then he said, I pray thee therefore, father, that thou wouldest **send him to my father's house**: —28 For **I have five brethren**; that he may **testify unto them**, lest they also come into this place of torment. —29 Abraham saith unto him, They have Moses and the prophets; let them hear them. —30 And he said, Nay, father Abraham: but if one went unto them from the dead, they will repent. —31 And he said unto him, If they hear not Moses and the prophets, neither will they be persuaded, though one rose from the dead. —Luke 16:19-31

- Carried by an angel to a designated location called Abraham's bosom (paradise).
- The rich man was being in torments in Hades in their spiritual body.
- He lifted **his eyes** and could **see (sight)** afar off on the other side toward paradise.
- The rich man cried and could speak (he also can display emotions, or emotional capacity).
- The rich man was conscience of his state of sin and convictions.
- Dip his **finger (touch and feel)** in water and cool his tongue (**taste**) in paradise because of the dryness and heat of Hades.
- He is tormented in the flame (**bodily feeling**).
- They can remember the history of their own pasts.
- Lazarus received comfort and the certain rich man experienced torment.
- Their spiritual bodies were confined to their appropriate locations by a great gulf fixed as boundary or hinderance.
- They can also have logical or future thinking for his other five brothers.

The five senses that humans are aware of are hearing, seeing, tasting, smelling, and touching. Your ability to detect odors enables you to experience flavors, as taste and smell are closely linked. In the spiritual realm, there are a multitude of scents and fragrances. If there is a flame burning, you will detect the unpleasant smell of burning flesh. God is a consuming fire, and His presence brings the Spirit of Burning.

SMELLING

As soon as I had the privilege of being baptized in water and receiving the Holy Spirit, I had a powerful encounter with the presence of God, which I could perceive through a distinct fragrance. In addition, I had the ability to detect various diseases such as cancer, among others.

FEELING (PHYSICAL)

And he cried and said, Father Abraham, have mercy on me, and send Lazarus, that he may dip the tip of his finger in water, and cool my tongue; for I am tormented in this flame. — Luke 16:24

TASTING

O taste and see that the LORD is good: blessed is the man that trusteth in him. —Psalms 34:8

MENTAL THOUGHTS, IMPRESSIONS, EMOTIONAL FEELINGS

Seeing and feeling would fall under most mental thoughts and or impressions. Most prophetic words come this way.

And this she did for many days. But Paul, <u>greatly annoyed</u>, turned and said to the spirit, "I command you in the name of Jesus Christ to come out of her." And he came out that very hour. — Act 16:18 NKJV

And this did she many days. But Paul, <u>being grieved</u>, turned and said to the spirit, I command thee in the name of Jesus Christ to come out of her. And he came out the same hour. —Acts 16:18 KJV

And Jesus, moved with compassion, put forth his hand, and touched him, and saith unto him, I will; be thou clean. —Mark 1:41

Reflections, Reviews, Questions

6. Meditate on the differences between the gift and the office (cited in the previous chart):

_____

_____

_____

_____

7. What do you think makes a prophet a gift to the church rather than just operating on the gift?

_____

_____

_____

8. Provide other scriptures or examples of instances showing that all believers can prophesy or that this is the will of the Lord:

_____

_____

_____

_____

_____

Notes

_____

_____

_____

_____

_____

_____

Gifts of the Holy Spirit

THE VOCAL GIFTS	THE REVELATORY GIFTS	THE POWER GIFTS
The Mouth of God	*The Mind of God*	*The Hand of God*
1. Diverse kinds of tongues	4. Discerning of spirits	7. Faith (Special Kind of Faith)
2. Interpretation of Tongues	5. (a)[1] word of knowledge	8. Diverse kinds of Healing (gifts)
3. Prophecy-foretell/forth tell	6. (a)[1] word of wisdom	9. Working of Miracles

TABLE 1 THE 3 CATEGORIES OF THE GIFTS OF THE HOLY SPIRIT

There are diversities of gifts, but the same Spirit. —1 Corinthians 12:4

But the manifestation of the Spirit is given to each one for the profit of all: —1 Corinthians 12:7

for to one is given the __word of wisdom__ through the Spirit, to another the __word of knowledge__ through the same Spirit, to another __faith__ by the same Spirit, to another __gifts of healings__ by the same Spirit, to another the __working of miracles__, to another __prophecy__, to another __discerning of spirits__, to another __different kinds of tongues__, to another the __interpretation of tongues__. But one and the same Spirit works all these things, distributing to each one individually as He wills. For as the body is one and has many members, but all the members of that one body, being many, are one body, so also is Christ. For by one Spirit we were all baptized into one body—whether Jews or Greeks, whether slaves or free—and __have all been made to drink into one Spirit__. —1 Corinthians 12:8-13

BUILD FAITH

So then faith cometh by hearing, and hearing by the word of God. — Romans 10:17

Working of Miracles
Diverse kinds of healings
Faith (special kind of faith)
a word of wisdom
a word of knowledge
Discerning of spirits
Prophecy-foretell/forthtell
Interpretation of Tongues
Diverse kinds of tongues

FIGURE 2 THE GIFTS LADDER

[1]*There is no definite article in Greek (the). The original and literal Greek translation is (a) Word of Wisdom*

To another the working of miracles; to another prophecy; to another discerning of spirits; to another divers kinds of tongues; to another the interpretation of tongues: —1 Corinthians 12:10

Reflections, Reviews, Questions

9. How does faith come from?

_____

_____

_____

10. What are the three categories of gifts in reference to the gifts of the Holy Spirit?

_____

_____

_____

_____

11. What are the secondary names of the three categories or what else can we call them?

_____

_____

_____

_____

12. Why are we referring to the word of knowledge as a word of knowledge instead?

_____

_____

_____

Notes

_____

_____

_____

_____

_____

The fruit (works) of the Spirit

καρπός | karpos **Thayer Definition**[3]:

1. Fruit
2. (**Work,** act, deed): that which originates or comes from something, an effect, result.

> But **the fruit** [work, deed, act] **of the Spirit** is love, joy, peace, longsuffering, gentleness, goodness, faith, —Galatians 5:22

> But if all prophesy, and there come in one that believeth not, or one unlearned, he is convinced of all, he is judged of all: —1 Corinthians 14:24

> Meekness, temperance: against such there is no law. —24 And they that are Christ's have crucified the flesh with the affections and lusts. —25 If we live in the Spirit, let us also walk in the Spirit. —26 Let us not be desirous of vain glory, provoking one another, envying one another. — Galatians 5:23-26

> For ye may all prophesy one by one, that all may learn, and all may be comforted. —1 Corinthians 14:31

> And the spirits of the prophets are subject to the prophets. —1 Corinthians 14:32
> For we know in part, and we prophesy in part. —1 Corinthians 13:9

Based on the context of Galatians 5:22, "works" is the more suitable translation, rather than "fruits." The Thayer definition includes two possible translation for the Greek word Karpos. The comparison between the works of flesh and those of the spirit realm becomes more evident when one reads the preceding scripture at Galatians 5:19-21.

> Now the works of the flesh are evident, which are: adultery, fornication, uncleanness, lewdness, idolatry, sorcery, hatred, contentions, jealousies, outbursts of wrath, selfish ambitions, dissensions, heresies, envy, murders, drunkenness, revelries, and the like; of which I tell you beforehand, just as I also told you in time past, that those who practice such things will not inherit the kingdom of God.
> —Galatians 5:19-21

Foundational Holiness is established upon the righteousness of Christ. We are considered righteous solely because of the grace that has been given to us. It is acquired positionally as being in Christ. We are holy because He is Holy. We are joined together with the Holy Spirit as one. Although we are holy positionally, there is a work we must do in order to maintain what as been given freely. Jesus, the High Priest, reveals to the seven churches in judgement that He is aware of their deeds or works. Our work will be tested by fire, for God is a consuming fire. The works of

---

[3] Thayer, *Thayer's Greek-English Lexicon of the New Testament.*

the spirit are the eternal works of love. Our inner character helps us maintain the operations of the gifts of the Holy Spirit. This is why is so important to have private victories in self-control.

Reflections, Reviews, Questions

13. Why is maintaining the fruit of the spirit as important as growing in the gifts? Can we have both or should we only push for one or the other?

_____

_____

_____

14. Do you believe it's necessary to maintain holiness in the Lord to have a more effective pure stream in the gifts?

_____

_____

_____

_____

15. Have you seen the Lord use someone with gifts, but their characters are not so great? What do you think about this?

_____

_____

_____

16. Do you believe these kinds of people will increase in their authority and power of their gifts if their fruit maturity increases along with their gift maturity?

_____

_____

_____

Notes

_____

_____

_____

_____

Prophesy according (proportion) to your faith

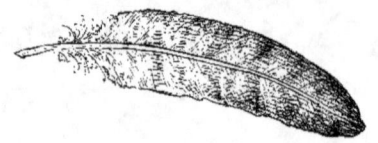

BURDEN OR WITNESS

*Having then gifts differing according to the grace that is given to us, whether prophecy, **let us prophesy according to the proportion of faith**; —Romans 12:6*

Once the assurance lifts, we need to stop prophesying. The presence of the Lord is the best litmus test in knowing when to stop. When you sense or discern that there is waning out of the presence of the Lord through the prophetic spirit—wrap it up and close your mouth.

Massa: the burden of the Lord, or when the hand of the Lord is upon you.

maśśâ' **'DB Definition:** Massa[4] = "bu"rden", load, bearing, tribute, burden, lifting ,utterance, oracle.

*The words of king Lemuel, the **prophecy** that his mother taught him. —**Proverb 31:1** NKJV*

The word "Massa" is mentioned in Proverb 31:1 of the Bible, and interestingly, it appears 65 times in the King James Version (KJV). Out of these occurrences, the majority, specifically 57 times, it has been translated as "burden." However, in this particular scripture, it has been translated as "prophecy" instead. The word "massa" is derived from the root word "naśa", which also signifies the actions of lifting, bearing up, carrying, and taking.

The burden of the word of the LORD in the land of Hadrach, and Damascus shall be the rest thereof: when the eyes of man, as of all the tribes of Israel, shall be toward the LORD. —Zechariah 9:1

The burden of the word of the LORD for Israel, saith the LORD, which stretcheth forth the heavens, and layeth the foundation of the earth, and formeth the spirit of man within him. —Zechariah 12:1

The burden of the word of the LORD to Israel by Malachi. —Malachi 1:1

Even though the specific Hebrew phrases for "Massa" or "burden" are not mentioned directly in these two verses, they hold similar prophetic implications. The description of this burden in Jeremiah 20:9 is vividly portrayed by Jeremiah as a burning fire that is trapped within his bones, fervently desiring to be set free. In Job 32:18-20, we encounter the story of Elihu, a young and wise individual whose passion for the Word of the Lord grew so intense

[4] Francis Brown, S. R. Driver, and Charles A. Briggs, *The Brown-Driver-Briggs Hebrew and English Lexicon*, Complete and Unabridged, fully searchable, with Strong Numbers and interactive Index edition (Peabody, Mass: Hendrickson Academic, 1994).

that he could no longer remain silent. As if the Word of the Lord had turned into a pressurized gas, he could feel its power building up in his stomach, waiting to be released and bring him a refreshing sensation.

> *Then I said, I will not make mention of him, nor speak any more in his name. But his word was in mine heart as a burning fire shut up in my bones, and I was weary with forbearing, and I could not stay. —Jeremiah 20:9*
>
> *For I am full of matter, the spirit within me constraineth me. Behold, my belly is as wine which hath no vent; it is ready to burst like new bottles. I will speak, that I may be refreshed: I will open my lips and answer. —Job 32:18-20*

Reflections, Reviews, Questions

17. What does "the burden of the Word of the Lord" mean in the context of the prophetic?

_____

_____

18. What is the Definition of Massa and Nassa? How are these related to the prophetic utterance?

_____

_____

_____

_____

19. Why is it important to prophesy according to the proportion of our own faith?

_____

_____

_____

20. Why is important to stop prophesying once we feel the burden of the Lord lift up?

_____

_____

_____

Notes

_____

_____

_____

_____

_____

_____

Desire to Prophesy

DESIRE TO PROPHESY.

Follow after charity, and ***desire*** *spiritual gifts, but* ***rather that ye may prophesy***. —1 Corinthians 14:1*

Pursue love, and desire spiritual gifts, but especially that you may prophesy. —1 Corinthians 14:1 NKJV

The number one thing that Paul states about spiritual gifts is to "Pursue Love" first and then "Desire" Spiritual gifts. Another way of looking at it is to first pursue "God" who is the giver of all the spiritual gifts. We go after the giver, keeping the first commandment first is the key to delve into the supernatural. He emphasizes that as we desire spiritual gifts, we would especially want to prophesy. One thing I love is a statement I heard from Dr. Stuart Pattico who says 'Desire' is a magnet that attracts the prophetic anointing." [6]

But he that prophesieth speaketh unto men to edification, and exhortation, and comfort. —1 Corinthians 14:3

I would that ye all spake with tongues, but rather that ye prophesied: for greater is he that prophesieth than he that speaketh with tongues, except he interpret, that the church may receive edifying. —1 Corinthians 14:5

Even so ye, forasmuch as ye are ***zealous*** *of spiritual gifts, seek that* ***ye may excel*** *to the edifying of the* ***church***. *—1 Corinthians 14:12*

Having then gifts differing according to the grace that is given to us, whether prophecy, ***let us prophesy according to the proportion of faith;***
—Romans 12:6b

---

5 Thomas Nelson, *NKJV, End-of-Verse Reference Bible, Personal Size Large Print, Leathersoft, Black, Red Letter, Comfort Print: Holy Bible, New King James Version,* Large type / Large print edition (Nashville: Thomas Nelson, 2020).

6 "How to Prophesy and Move in the Prophetic," Dr. Stuart Pattico, accessed March 22, 2022, http://www.stuartpattico.com/2/post/2017/04/how-to-prophesy-and-move-in-the-prophetic.html.

*For I say, through the grace given unto me, to every man that is among you, not to think of himself more highly than he ought to think; but to think soberly, according as **God hath dealt to every man the measure of faith.** —Romans 12:3*

WHY WE MUST PURSUE LOVE?

Pursue love, <u>and</u> desire spiritual gifts, —1 Corinthians 14:1a NKJV

And Enoch lived sixty and five years, and begat Methuselah: — 22 And Enoch walked with God after he begat Methuselah three hundred years, and begat sons and daughters: — 23 And all the days of Enoch were three hundred sixty and five years: — 24 And Enoch walked with God: and he was not; for God took him.—Genesis 5:21-24 KJV

Enoch means to instruct or to initiate, but it also means dedicated, consecrated, and experienced.

Walking with God: "to walk habitually up and down in conversation with God. He was in constant fellowship with God."[7]

*__Who shall ascend into the hill of the LORD__? or who shall **stand** in his holy place? — 4 He that hath **clean hands**, and **a pure heart**; who hath **not lifted up his soul** unto vanity, nor **sworn deceitfully**. — 5 He shall receive the **blessing** from the LORD, and **righteousness** from the God of his salvation. — 6 This is the generation of them that **seek him**, that **seek thy face**, O Jacob. Selah. —7 Lift up your heads, O ye gates; and be ye lift up, ye everlasting doors; and the King of glory shall come in. —8 Who is this King of glory? The LORD strong and mighty, the LORD mighty in battle. —9 Lift up your heads, O ye **gates**; even lift them up, ye everlasting **doors**; and the King of glory shall come in. —10 Who is this King of glory? The LORD of hosts, he is the King of glory. Selah.—Psalms 24:3-10*

Submit yourselves therefore to God. Resist the devil, and he will flee from you. —8 Draw nigh to God, and he will draw nigh to you. Cleanse your hands, ye sinners; and purify your hearts, ye double minded.— James 4:7-8

PURPOSE IN YOUR HEART TO RECEIVE

*But <u>Daniel</u> **purposed in his heart** <u>that he would not defile himself</u> with the portion of the king's meat, nor with the wine which he drank: therefore he requested of the prince of the eunuchs that he might not defile himself. —Daniel 1:8*

*Follow after charity, <u>and</u> **desire** spiritual gifts, but **rather that ye may prophesy**. —1 Corinthians 14:1*

__Pursue love__, and desire spiritual gifts, but especially that you may prophesy. —1 Corinthians 14:1[8] NKJV

---

[7] Sundar Selvaraj, *Wait As Eagles* (Jesus Ministries, 2015).

[8] Nelson, *NKJV, End-of-Verse Reference Bible, Personal Size Large Print, Leathersoft, Black, Red Letter, Comfort Print.*

The Love of God should take precedence for ministers exploring the supernatural lifestyle. The Love of God is what enables you to stay consistent in ministering to God and people for decades. The exercise of the gifts is fueled by the passionate Love of God. When your love for the people you minister to fades, your ministry loses its purpose. The church is admonished by Apostle Paul to prioritize purpose and compassion for people in the love of God. Above everything else, we must prioritize loving God and loving people. Gifts won't be needed in the next era, but God's love will remain eternal. The gifts are provided to destroy the work of the adversary for loving others externally. To develop our internal character, each believer must be perfected in the love of God.

Reflections, Reviews, Questions

21. What is the connection between the "desire" of the gift of prophecy and walking in the gift of prophecy?

_____

_____

22. What did Daniel purposed in his heart to do in order to walk in the supernatural?

_____

_____

23. Using the power of substitution, can you just say that pursuing love means to pursue God?

_____

_____

24. How do you walk with God like Enoch?

_____

_____

_____

25. Who shall ascend into the hill of the Lord and how do you do that?

_____

_____

_____

26. What is more important to God, gifts, or character? Are we able to maintain both?

_____

_____

Notes

_____

_____

_____

The Gift of Prophecy and Laying on of hands

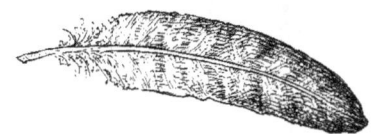

*And though I have the <u>gift of prophecy</u>, and **understand all mysteries** and **all knowledge**, and though I have all faith, so that I could remove mountains, but have not love, I am nothing. —1 Corinthians 13:2*

Though <u>I speak</u> with the <u>tongues of men</u> and <u>of angels</u>, and have not charity, I am become as sounding brass, or a tinkling cymbal.—1 Corinthians 13:1

And though <u>I bestow all my goods to feed the poor</u>, and though <u>I give my body to be burned</u>, and have not charity, it profiteth me nothing.—1 Corinthians 13:3

GIFT OF PROPHECY

*Do not neglect the gift that is in you, which was given to you by **prophecy** with the <u>laying on of the hands of the eldership</u>. —1 Timothy 4:14*

I wish you all spoke with tongues, but even more that you prophesied; for he who prophesies is greater than he who speaks with tongues, unless indeed he interprets, that the church may receive edification.—1 Corinthians 14:5

In 1 Timothy 4:14, Paul instructs Timothy to not neglect the gift that was given to him through the laying on of hands by the elders. This passage reveals the importance of impartation, where the older generation transfers their spiritual authority and anointing to the younger generation. The act of laying on of hands signifies the transference of power and authority, with the release of prophetic words by the presbytery confirms and activates the gifts for the one receiving. This process is crucial for the development and activation of the gifts and calling in the younger generations, as it connects them to the spiritual heritage and empowers them to walk in their God-given purpose.

The gift of prophecy, as stated in 1 Corinthians 13:2, is the ability to comprehend mysteries and knowledge. It is based on revelation and understanding the Word of God. By studying and acquiring knowledge, we can enhance this gift.

Reflections, Reviews, Questions

27. Gifts are given or imparted via what two structures per 1 Timothy 4:14?

_____

_____

_____

28. If the maximization of the gift of faith is to remove a mountain, what is the maximization of the gift of prophecy?

_____

_____

_____

29. Besides personal prophecy, as outlined in 1 Corinthians 13:2, what other essential operation serves as the foundation for the gift of prophecy?

_____

_____

_____

Notes

_____

_____

_____

_____

_____

_____

_____

_____

Prophecy and Tongues

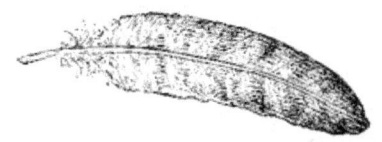

Follow after charity, and desire spiritual gifts, but rather that ye may prophesy. —2 For he that speaketh in an unknown tongue speaketh not unto men, but unto God: for no man understandeth him; howbeit in the spirit he speaketh mysteries. —3 But he that prophesieth speaketh unto men to edification, and exhortation, and comfort. —4 He that speaketh in an unknown tongue edifieth himself; but he that prophesieth edifieth the church. —5 I would that ye all spake with tongues, but rather that ye prophesied: for greater is he that prophesieth than he that speaketh with tongues, except he interpret, that the church may receive edifying. —6 Now, brethren, if I come unto you speaking with tongues, what shall I profit you, except I shall speak to you either by revelation, or by knowledge, or by prophesying, or by doctrine? —7 And even things without life giving sound, whether pipe or harp, except they give a distinction in the sounds, how shall it be known what is piped or harped? —8 For if the trumpet give an uncertain sound, who shall prepare himself to the battle? —9 So likewise ye, except ye utter by the tongue words easy to be understood, how shall it be known what is spoken? for ye shall speak into the air. —10 There are, it may be, so many kinds of voices in the world, and none of them is without signification. —11 Therefore if I know not the meaning of the voice, I shall be unto him that speaketh a barbarian, and he that speaketh shall be a barbarian unto me. —12 Even so ye, forasmuch as ye are zealous of spiritual gifts, seek that ye may excel to the edifying of the church. —13 Wherefore let him that speaketh in an unknown tongue pray that he may interpret. —14 For if I pray in an unknown tongue, my spirit prayeth, but my understanding is unfruitful. —15 What is it then? I will pray with the spirit, and I will pray with the understanding also: I will sing with the spirit, and I will sing with the understanding also. —16 Else when thou shalt bless with the spirit, how shall he that occupieth the room of the unlearned say Amen at thy giving of thanks, seeing he understandeth not what thou sayest? —17 For thou verily givest thanks well, but the other is not edified. —18 I thank my God, I speak with tongues more than ye all: —19 Yet in the church I had rather speak five words with my understanding, that by my voice I might teach others also, than ten thousand words in an unknown tongue. —20 Brethren, be not children in understanding: howbeit in malice be ye children, but in understanding be men. —21 In the law it is written, With men of other tongues and other lips will I speak unto this people; and yet for all that will they not hear me, saith the Lord. —22 Wherefore tongues are for a sign, not to them that believe, but to them that believe not: but prophesying serveth not for them that believe not, but for them which believe. —23 If therefore the whole church be come together into one place, and all speak with tongues, and there come in those that are unlearned, or unbelievers, will they not say that ye are mad? —24 But if all prophesy, and there come in one that believeth not, or one unlearned, he is convinced of all, he is judged of all: —25 And thus are the secrets of his heart made manifest; and so falling down on his face he will worship God, and report that God is in you of a truth. —1 Corinthians 14:1-25

WHEN THE SPIRIT OF THE LORD CAME UPON THEM THEY PROPHESIED AND SPOKE IN TONGUES

*And when Paul had laid his hands upon them, the Holy Ghost came on them; and **they spake with tongues, and prophesied.** —Acts 19:6*

When the Spirit of the Lord came upon them through impartation or preaching, their response would be either tongues or prophecy. Prophecy has been evidence of God's true presence since the Old Testament. The sole distinction within the New Testament lies in the inclusion of the act of speaking in the most holy faith—tongues. It is a logical progression that tongues and interpretations of tongues would give way to prophecy. This is actually another way to access the prophetic through interpreting tongues. The use of tongues is advantageous solely to the speaker unless there is interpretation, in which case it benefits the entire congregation.

*And it came to pass, that, while Apollos was at Corinth, Paul having passed through the upper coasts came to Ephesus: and finding certain disciples, —2 He said unto them, Have ye received the Holy Ghost since ye believed? And they said unto him, We have not so much as heard whether there be any Holy Ghost. —3 And he said unto them, Unto what then were ye baptized? And they said, Unto John's baptism. —4 Then said Paul, John verily baptized with the baptism of repentance, saying unto the people, that they should believe on him which should come after him, that is, on Christ Jesus. —5 <u>When they heard this, they were baptized in the name of the Lord Jesus.</u> —6 And when <u>Paul had laid his hands upon them, the Holy Ghost came on them</u>; and **they spake with tongues, and prophesied**. —7 And all the men were about twelve.—Acts 19:1-7*

It can be observed that subsequent to being baptized in Jesus and receiving the laying on of hands by the presbytery, they commenced speaking in tongues and engaging in prophetic utterances.

*And Saul sent messengers to take David: and when they saw the company of the prophets prophesying, and Samuel standing as appointed over them, <u>the Spirit of God was upon the messengers of Saul</u>, and **they also prophesied**. —21 And when it was told Saul, he sent other messengers, and **they prophesied likewise.** And Saul sent messengers again the third time, and **they prophesied also**. —22 Then went he also to Ramah, and came to a great well that is in Sechu: and he asked and said, Where are Samuel and David? And one said, Behold, they be at Naioth in Ramah. —23 And he went thither to Naioth in Ramah: and the <u>Spirit of God was upon him also</u>, and **he went on, and prophesied**, until he came to Naioth in Ramah. —24 And he stripped off his clothes also, and **prophesied before Samuel in like manner**, and lay down naked all that day and all that night. Wherefore they say, Is Saul also among the prophets? —1 Samuel 19:20-24*

After that thou shalt come to the hill of God, where is the garrison of the Philistines: and it shall come to pass, when thou art come thither to the city, that <u>thou shalt meet a company of prophets</u> coming down from the high place with a psaltery, and a tabret, and a pipe, and a harp, before them; and they shall prophesy: —6 And <u>the Spirit of the LORD will come upon thee</u>, and <u>thou shalt prophesy with them</u>, and <u>shalt be turned into another man</u>. —7 And let it be, when these signs are come unto thee, that thou do *as occasion serve thee; for God is with thee. —8 And thou shalt go down before me to Gilgal; and, behold, I will come down unto thee, to offer burnt offerings, and to sacrifice sacrifices of peace offerings: seven days shalt thou tarry, till I come to thee, and shew thee what thou shalt do. —9 And it was so, that when he had turned his back to go from Samuel, <u>God gave him another heart</u>: and all those signs came to pass that day. —10 And when they came thither to the hill, behold, a company of prophets met him; and <u>the Spirit of God came upon him</u>, and **he prophesied among them**. —11 And it came to pass, when all that knew him beforetime saw that, behold, **he prophesied among the prophets**, then the people said one to another, What is this that is come unto the son of Kish? Is Saul also among the prophets? —1 Samuel 10:5-11*

*Then **the Spirit of God came upon Zechariah** the son of Jehoiada the priest, who stood above the people, and said to them, "**Thus says God:** 'Why do you transgress the commandments of the LORD, so that you cannot prosper? Because you have forsaken the LORD, He also has forsaken you.'" —21 So they conspired against him, and at the command of the king they stoned him with stones in the court of the house of the LORD. —22 Thus Joash the king did not remember the kindness which Jehoiada his father had done to him, but killed his son; and as he died, he said, "The LORD look on it, and repay!" —23 So it happened in the spring of the year that the army of Syria came up against him; and they came to Judah and Jerusalem, and destroyed all the leaders of the people from among the people, and sent all their spoil to the king of Damascus. — 2 Chronicles 24:20-23 NKJV*

*And all Judah stood before the LORD, with their little ones, their wives, and their children. —14 **Then upon Jahaziel** the son of Zechariah, the son of Benaiah, the son of Jeiel, the son of Mattaniah, a Levite of the sons of Asaph, **came the Spirit of the LORD** in the midst of the congregation; —15 And he said, Hearken ye, all Judah, and ye inhabitants of Jerusalem, and thou king Jehoshaphat, **Thus saith the LORD** unto you, Be not afraid nor dismayed by reason of this great multitude; for the battle is not yours, but God's. —16 Tomorrow go ye down against them: behold, they come up by the cliff of Ziz; and ye shall find them at the end of the brook, before the wilderness of Jeruel. —17 Ye shall not need to fight in this battle: set yourselves, stand ye still, and see the salvation of the LORD with you, O Judah and Jerusalem: fear not, nor be dismayed; tomorrow go out against them: for the LORD will be with you. —18 And Jehoshaphat bowed his head with his face to the ground: and all Judah and the inhabitants of Jerusalem fell before the LORD, worshipping the LORD. —19 And the Levites, of the children of the Kohathites, and of the children of the Korhites, stood up to praise the LORD God of Israel with a loud voice on high. —20 And they rose early in the morning, and went forth into the wilderness of Tekoa: and as they went forth, Jehoshaphat stood and said, Hear me, O Judah, and ye inhabitants of Jerusalem; Believe in the LORD your God, so shall ye be established; <u>believe his prophets, so shall ye prosper.</u> —21 And when he had consulted with the people, he appointed singers unto the LORD, and that should praise the beauty of holiness, as they went out before the army, and to say, Praise the LORD; for his mercy endureth for ever. —22 And when they began to sing and to praise, the LORD set ambushments against the children of Ammon, Moab, and mount Seir, which were come against Judah; and they were smitten. —2 Chronicles 20:13-22*

*And they made signs to his father, how he would have him called. —63 And he asked for a writing table, and wrote, saying, His name is John. And they marvelled all. —64 **And his mouth was opened immediately, and his tongue loosed, and he spake, and praised God.** —Luke 1:62-64*

*And his father Zacharias **was filled with the Holy Ghost, and prophesied, saying**, —68 Blessed be the Lord God of Israel; for he hath visited and redeemed his people, —69 And hath raised up an horn of salvation for us in the house of his servant David; —70 As he spake by the mouth of his holy prophets, which have been since the world began: —71 That we should be saved from our enemies, and from the hand of all that hate us; —72 To perform the mercy promised to our fathers, and to remember his holy covenant; —73 The oath which he sware to our father Abraham, —74 That he would grant unto us, that we being delivered out of the hand of our enemies might serve him without fear, —75 In holiness and righteousness before him, all the days of our life. —76 And thou, child, shalt be called the prophet of the Highest: for thou shalt go before the face of the Lord to prepare his ways; —77 To give knowledge of salvation unto his people by the remission of their sins, —78 Through the tender mercy of our God; whereby the dayspring from on high hath visited us, —79 To give light to them that sit in darkness and in the shadow of death, to guide our feet into the way of peace. —80 And the child grew, and waxed strong in spirit, and was in the deserts till the day of his shewing unto Israel. —Luke 1:67-80*

*And it came to pass, that, when Elisabeth heard the salutation of Mary, the babe leaped in her womb; and **Elisabeth was filled with the Holy Ghost**: —42 And she spake out with a loud voice, and said, Blessed art thou among women, and blessed is the fruit of thy womb. —43 And whence is this to me, that the mother of my Lord should come to me? —44 For, lo, as soon as the voice of thy salutation sounded in mine ears, the babe leaped in my womb for joy. —45 And blessed is she that believed: for there shall be a performance of those things which were told her from the Lord. —Luke 1:41-45*

In Job 32, Elihu explains how the prophetic word came to him and the internal process that occurs when it happens. He compares it to a new wineskin bursting, seeking release. It's similar to uncorking a wine bottle when the Spirit of the Lord comes upon you. Your belly is filled with praises and prophetic messages from the Lord, and in order to find relief, you must prophesy. This is akin to the scripture's description of the roar of a lion.

*For **I am full of matter, the spirit within me constraineth me.** —19 Behold, my belly is as wine which hath no vent; it is ready to burst like new bottles. —20 I will speak, that I may be refreshed: I will open my lips and answer. —Job 32:18-20*

Consequently, we must avoid suppressing or quenching the Spirit of the Lord when we are burdened by His presence. We must prophesy by either writing and recording down the prophetic word and if protocol from leadership approves it should be released to the people in the meeting.

*Quench not the Spirit. **Despise not prophesyings.** —1 Thessalonians 5:19-20*

Reflections, Reviews, Questions

30. When you have tongues and interpretation working together what do you have?

_____

_____

31. Explain the "Diverse" kinds of tongues which we know so far as part of the gift of tongues.

_____

_____

_____

32. In the Old Testament when the presence of the Lord came upon them what did they do and what was manifested? In the New Testament there is an additional manifestation, what is it?

_____

_____

_____

_____

Notes

_____

_____

_____

_____

_____

_____

_____

Prophetic Anointing is Contagious

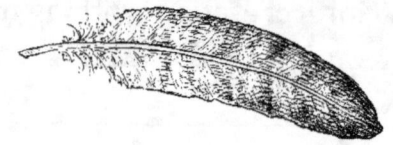

*After that thou shalt come to the hill of God, where is the garrison of the Philistines: and it shall come to pass, when thou art come thither to the city, that **thou shalt meet a company of prophets** coming down from the high place with a psaltery, and a tabret, and a pipe, and a harp, before them; and <u>they shall prophesy</u>: —6 And <u>the Spirit of the LORD will come upon thee</u>, and <u>thou shalt prophesy with them</u>, and <u>shalt be turned into another man.</u> —7 And let it be, when these signs are come unto thee, that thou do as occasion serve thee; for God is with thee. —8 And thou shalt go down before me to Gilgal; and, behold, I will come down unto thee, to offer burnt offerings, and to sacrifice sacrifices of peace offerings: seven days shalt thou tarry, till I come to thee, and shew thee what thou shalt do. —9 And it was so, that when he had turned his back to go from Samuel, <u>God gave him another heart</u>: and all those signs came to pass that day. —10 And when they came thither to the hill, behold, <u>a company of prophets met him;</u> and <u>the Spirit of God came upon him, and he prophesied among them.</u> —11 And it came to pass, when all that knew him beforetime saw that, behold, <u>he prophesied among the prophets</u>, then the people said one to another, What is this that is come unto the son of Kish? Is Saul also among the prophets? —12 And one of the same place answered and said, But who is their father? Therefore it became a proverb, Is Saul also among the prophets? —13 And when he had made an end of prophesying, he came to the high place. —14 And Saul's uncle said unto him and to his servant, Whither went ye? And he said, To seek the asses: and when we saw that they were no where, we came to Samuel. —15 And Saul's uncle said, Tell me, I pray thee, what Samuel said unto you. —16 And Saul said unto his uncle, He told us plainly that the asses were found. But of the matter of the kingdom, whereof Samuel spake, he told him not. — 1 Samuel 10:5-16*

There is something that happens when you are prophesying with a company of prophets or prophetic teams. In my perspective, there appears to be a somewhat intangible vortex that exerts influence over the entire group. When you are surrounded by prophetic individuals, it becomes easier to prophesy. There is an exponential increase in the multiplication of the prophetic anointing. By engaging in this practice, individuals who are just beginning to prophesy are able to elevate their abilities to a higher level than before. This is achieved through the acquisition of gifts that are present within the group, facilitated by impartation. Witnessing this is an absolute marvel and a sight to behold. The scripture provided above highlights the remarkable transformation of Saul, who was completely changed into a different individual as a direct result of being immersed in the prophetic anointing.

Reflections, Reviews, Questions

33. Why is the Prophetic Anointing so contagious?

_____

_____

_____

34. Who does the Prophetic anointing belong to, anyway?

_____

_____

_____

35. Why is it easier to prophesy in a company of prophets?

Notes

_____

_____

_____

_____

_____

_____

_____

_____

_____

Different Prophetic Expressions

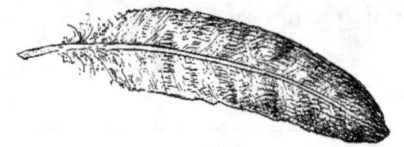

CULTIVATING THE PROPHETIC THROUGH WORSHIP AND PRAISE

PROPHESYING WITH THE HARP

Moreover David and the captains of the host separated to the service of the sons of Asaph, and of Heman, and of Jeduthun, who should prophesy with harps, with psalteries, and with cymbals: and the number of the workmen according to their service was: —2 Of the sons of Asaph; Zaccur, and Joseph, and Nethaniah, and Asarelah, the sons of Asaph under the hands of Asaph, which prophesied according to the order of the king.   —3 Of Jeduthun: the sons of Jeduthun; Gedaliah, and Zeri, and Jeshaiah, Hashabiah, and Mattithiah, six, under the hands of their father Jeduthun, who prophesied with a harp, to give thanks and to praise the LORD. –1 Chronicles 25:1-3

THE NEW SONG OF THE LORD

Singing a new song to the Lord always brings an increase in the prophetic anointing in a congregation. This is one of the quicksets way to activate prophetic teams or new people into the prophetic. This type of activation doesn't matter if the persons involved don't even know how to sing. This is all about the heart of worship and living a lifestyle of obedience. Refer to the School of the Holy Spirit Manual 1 "Worship the Lord in the beauty of holiness!"

O sing unto the LORD a new song: sing unto the LORD, all the earth.   —2 Sing unto the LORD, bless his name; shew forth his salvation from day to day.   —3 Declare his glory among the heathen, his wonders among all people.   —4 For the LORD is great, and greatly to be praised: he is to be feared above all gods.   —5 For all the gods of the nations are idols: but the LORD made the heavens.   —6 Honour and majesty are before him: strength and beauty are in his sanctuary.   —7 Give unto the LORD, O ye kindreds of the people, give unto the LORD glory and strength.   —8 Give unto the LORD the glory due unto his name: bring an offering, and come into his courts.   —9 O worship the LORD in the beauty of holiness: fear before him, all the earth.   —10 Say among the heathen that the LORD reigneth: the world also shall be established that it shall not be moved: he shall judge the people righteously.   —11 Let the heavens rejoice, and let the earth be glad; let the sea roar, and the fulness thereof.   —12 Let the field be joyful, and all that is therein: then shall all the trees of the wood rejoice   —13 Before the LORD: for he cometh, for he cometh to judge the earth: he shall judge the world with righteousness, and the people with his truth.— Psalms 96:1-13

PROPHETIC DANCE

> *Let them praise his name in the dance: let them sing praises unto him with the timbrel and harp. —Psalms 149:3*

PROPHETIC PRAYER

> *He that dwelleth in the secret place of the most High shall abide under the shadow of the Almighty. I will say of the LORD, He is my refuge and my fortress: my God; in him will I trust. Surely he shall deliver thee from the snare of the fowler, and from the noisome pestilence. He shall cover thee with his feathers, and under his wings shalt thou trust: his truth shall be thy shield and buckler. Thou shalt not be afraid for the terror by night; nor for the arrow that flieth by day; Nor for the pestilence that walketh in darkness; nor for the destruction that wasteth at noonday. A thousand shall fall at thy side, and ten thousand at thy right hand; but it shall not come nigh thee. Only with thine eyes shalt thou behold and see the reward of the wicked. Because thou hast made the LORD, which is my refuge, even the most High, thy habitation; There shall no evil befall thee, neither shall any plague come nigh thy dwelling.—Psalms 91:1-10*

> *I have set the LORD always before me: because he is at my right hand, I shall not be moved. Therefore my heart is glad, and my glory rejoiceth: my flesh also shall rest in hope. For thou wilt not leave my soul in hell; neither wilt thou suffer thine Holy One to see corruption. Thou wilt shew me the path of life: in thy presence is fulness of joy; at thy right hand there are pleasures for evermore. —Psalms 16:8-11*

Praying with prophetic insight. As you engage in prayer for someone, remember to cover specific areas in your prayers. Most people pray prophetically and yet don't even realize that they are being prophetic. They believe that all they are doing is praying. Those who pray in this manner are more proficient in the prophetic flow of the Nabiy style. Their Nabiy senses have developed faster, allowing them to begin prophesying quicker in the Nabiy flow.

PROPHETIC ACT OR ACTION

> *And as we tarried there many days, there came down from Judaea a certain prophet, named Agabus. — 11 And when he was come unto us, he took Paul's girdle, and bound his own hands and feet, and said, thus saith the Holy Ghost, So shall the Jews at Jerusalem bind the man that owneth this girdle, and shall deliver him into the hands of the Gentiles. — Acts 21:10-11*

PROPHETIC PARABLE

PROPHET NATHAN WITH A PARABLE DAVID TO A RICH MAN'S LAMB
A comparison liken to another

And the LORD sent Nathan unto David. And he came unto him, and said unto him, There were two men in one city; the one rich, and the other poor. —2 The rich man had exceeding many flocks and herds: —3 But the poor man had nothing, save one little ewe lamb, which he had bought and nourished up: and it grew up together with him, and with his children; it did eat of his own meat, and drank of his own cup, and lay in his bosom, and was unto him as a daughter. —4 And there came a traveller unto the rich man, and he spared to take of his own flock and of his own herd, to dress for the wayfaring man that was come unto him; but took the poor man's lamb, and dressed it for the man that was come to him. —5 And David's anger was greatly kindled against the man; and he said to Nathan, As the LORD liveth, the man that hath done this thing shall surely die: —6 And he shall restore the lamb fourfold, because he did this thing, and because he had no pity. —7 And Nathan said to David, Thou art the man. Thus saith the LORD God of Israel, I anointed thee king over Israel, and I delivered thee out of the hand of Saul; —8 And I gave thee thy master's house, and thy master's wives into thy bosom, and gave thee the house of Israel and of Judah; and if that had been too little, I would moreover have given unto thee such and such things. —9 Wherefore hast thou despised the commandment of the LORD, to do evil in his sight? thou hast killed Uriah the Hittite with the sword, and hast taken his wife to be thy wife, and hast slain him with the sword of the children of Ammon. —10 Now therefore the sword shall never depart from thine house; because thou hast despised me, and hast taken the wife of Uriah the Hittite to be thy wife. —11 Thus saith the LORD, Behold, I will raise up evil against thee out of thine own house, and I will take thy wives before thine eyes, and give them unto thy neighbour, and he shall lie with thy wives in the sight of this sun. —12 For thou didst it secretly: but I will do this thing before all Israel, and before the sun. —13 And David said unto Nathan, I have sinned against the LORD. And Nathan said unto David, The LORD also hath put away thy sin; thou shalt not die. —14 Howbeit, because by this deed thou hast given great occasion to the enemies of the LORD to blaspheme, the child also that is born unto thee shall surely die. — 2 Samuel 12:1-14

PROPHETIC SONG

In that day shall this song be sung in the land of Judah; We have a strong city; salvation will God appoint for walls and bulwarks. Open ye the gates, that the righteous nation which keepeth the truth may enter in. Thou wilt keep him in perfect peace, whose mind is stayed on thee: because he trusteth in thee. Trust ye in the LORD for ever: for in the LORD JEHOVAH is everlasting strength: —Isaiah 26:1-4

And he hath put a new song in my mouth, even praise unto our God: many shall see it, and fear, and shall trust in the LORD. —Psalms 40:3

PROPHETIC PREACHING, TEACHING, OR REVEALING MYSTERIES

Peter's Sermon at Pentecost

But Peter, standing up with the eleven, lifted up his voice, and said unto them, Ye men of Judaea, and all ye that dwell at Jerusalem, be this known unto you, and hearken to my words: —15 For these are not drunken, as ye suppose, seeing it is but the third hour of the day. —16 But this is that which was spoken by the prophet Joel; —17 And it shall come to pass in the last days, saith God, I will pour out of my Spirit upon all flesh: and your sons and your daughters shall prophesy, and your young men shall see visions, and your old men shall dream dreams: —18 And on my servants and on my handmaidens I will pour out in those days of my Spirit; and they shall prophesy: —19 And I will shew wonders in heaven above, and signs in the earth beneath; blood, and fire, and vapour of smoke: —20 The sun shall be turned into darkness, and the moon into blood, before that great and notable day of the Lord come: —21 And it shall come to pass, that whosoever shall call on the name of the Lord shall be saved. —22 Ye men of Israel, hear these words; Jesus of Nazareth, a man approved of God among you by miracles and wonders and signs, which God did by him in the midst of you, as ye yourselves also know: —23 Him, being delivered by the determinate counsel and foreknowledge of God, ye have taken, and by wicked hands have crucified and slain: —24 Whom God hath raised up, having loosed the pains of death: because it was not possible that he should be holden of it. —25 For David speaketh concerning him, I foresaw the Lord always before my face, for he is on my right hand, that I should not be moved: —26 Therefore did my heart rejoice, and my tongue was glad; moreover also my flesh shall rest in hope: —27 Because thou wilt not leave my soul in hell, neither wilt thou suffer thine Holy One to see corruption. —28 Thou hast made known to me the ways of life; thou shalt make me full of joy with thy countenance. —29 Men and brethren, let me freely speak unto you of the patriarch David, that he is both dead and buried, and his sepulchre is with us unto this day. —30 Therefore being a prophet, and knowing that God had sworn with an oath to him, that of the fruit of his loins, according to the flesh, he would raise up Christ to sit on his throne; —31 He seeing this before spake of the resurrection of Christ, that his soul was not left in hell, neither his flesh did see corruption. —32 This Jesus hath God raised up, whereof we all are witnesses. —33 Therefore being by the right hand of God exalted, and having received of the Father the promise of the Holy Ghost, he hath shed forth this, which ye now see and hear. —34 For David is not ascended into the heavens: but he saith himself, The LORD said unto my Lord, Sit thou on my right hand, —35 Until I make thy foes thy footstool. —36 Therefore let all the house of Israel know assuredly, that God hath made that same Jesus, whom ye have crucified, both Lord and Christ. —37 Now when they heard this, they were pricked in their heart, and said unto Peter and to the rest of the apostles, Men and brethren, what shall we do? —38 Then Peter said unto them, Repent, and be baptized every one of you in the name of Jesus Christ for the remission of sins, and ye shall receive the gift of the Holy Ghost. —39 For the promise is unto you, and to your children, and to all that are afar off, even as many as the Lord our God shall call. —40 And with many other words did he testify and exhort, saying, Save yourselves from this untoward generation. —41 Then they that gladly received his word were baptized: and the same day there were added unto them about three thousand souls. —Acts 2:14-41

If any man speak, let him speak as the oracles of God; if any man minister, let him do it as of the ability which God giveth: that God in all things may be glorified through Jesus Christ, to whom be praise and dominion for ever and ever. Amen. —1 Peter 4:11

Now ye are the body of Christ, and members in particular. —28 And God hath set some in the church, first apostles, secondarily prophets, thirdly teachers, after that miracles, then gifts of healings, helps, governments, diversities of tongues. —29 Are all apostles? are all prophets? are all teachers? are all workers of miracles? —30 Have all the gifts of healing? do all speak with tongues? do all interpret? —31 But covet earnestly the best gifts: and yet shew I unto you a more excellent way.—1 Corinthians 12:27-31

Reflections, Reviews, Questions

36. Can the prophetic gift be expressed in different ways? If so please list several ways?

_____

_____

_____

37. What does a crafted or prepared prayer look like?

_____

_____

_____

38. Tell us what you think about Peter's sermon and how it could exemplify prophetic preaching:

_____

_____

_____

39. What is a biblical example of a prophetic song? How do you cultivate the prophetic through worship?

_____

_____

_____

Notes

_____

_____

_____

_____

How to test (judge) a prophetic word?

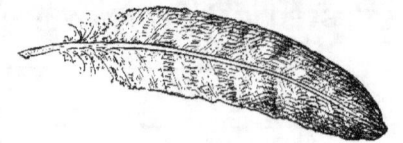

FOUR KEY POINTS

The following key points below will open up important questions in order to reveal the truth and motive of a prophetic word. Ask these questions to judge the prophecy?

DOES THE PROPHECY **LEAD** YOU CLOSER TO JESUS?

- WHEN IT'S A PREDICTION OR A PROPHETIC WORD, DOES IT COME TRUE WHEN THE CONDITIONS ARE MET?

- SOME PROPHECIES ARE CONDITIONALS (JONAH'S PROPHECY DIDN'T COME TO PASS BECAUSE THEY REPENTED)

- DOES THIS CONTRADICT WHAT THE LORD TOLD YOU PERSONALLY?

A Man of God Confronts Jeroboam

And behold, a man of God went from Judah to Bethel by the word of the LORD, and Jeroboam stood by the altar to burn incense. Then he cried out against the altar by the word of the LORD, and said, "O altar, altar! Thus says the LORD: 'Behold, a child, Josiah by name, shall be born to the house of David; and on you he shall sacrifice the priests of the high places who burn incense on you, and men's bones shall be burned on you.'" And he gave a sign the same day, saying, "This is the sign which the LORD has spoken: Surely the altar shall split apart, and the ashes on it shall be poured out." So it came to pass when King Jeroboam heard the saying of the man of God, who cried out against the altar in Bethel, that he stretched out his hand from the altar, saying, "Arrest him!" Then his hand, which he stretched out toward him, withered, so that he could not pull it back to himself. The altar also was split apart, and the ashes poured out from the altar, according to the sign which the man of God had given by the word of the LORD. Then the king answered and said to the man of God, "Please entreat the favor of the LORD your God, and pray for me, that my hand may be restored to me." So the man of God entreated the LORD, and the king's hand was restored to him, and became as before. Then the king said to the man of God, "Come home with me and refresh yourself, and I will give you a reward." But the man of God said to the king, "If you were to give me half your house, I would not go in with you; nor would I eat bread nor drink water in this place. For so it was commanded me by the word of the LORD, saying, 'You shall not eat bread, nor drink water, nor return by the same way you came.'" So he went another way and did not return by the way he came to Bethel.—1 Kings 13:1-10

The Prophet's Disobedience

Now an old prophet dwelt in Bethel, and his sons came and told him all the works that the man of God had done that day in Bethel; they also told their father the words which he had spoken to the king. And their father said to them, "Which way did he go?" For his sons had seen which way the man of God went who came from Judah. Then he said to his sons, "Saddle the donkey for me." So they saddled the donkey for him; and he rode on it, and went after the man of God, and found him sitting under an oak. Then he said to him, "Are you the man of God who came from Judah?" And he said, "I am." Then he said to him, "Come home with me and eat bread." And he said, "I cannot return with you nor go in with you; neither can I eat bread nor drink water with you in this place. For I have been told by the word of the LORD, 'You shall not eat bread nor drink water there, nor return by going the way you came.' " He said to him, "I too am a prophet as you are, and an angel spoke to me by the word of the LORD, saying, 'Bring him back with you to your house, that he may eat bread and drink water.' " (He was lying to him.) So he went back with him, and ate bread in his house, and drank water. Now it happened, as they sat at the table, that the word of the LORD came to the prophet who had brought him back; and he cried out to the man of God who came from Judah, saying, "Thus says the LORD: 'Because you have disobeyed the word of the LORD, and have not kept the commandment which the LORD your God commanded you, but you came back, ate bread, and drank water in the place of which the LORD said to you, "Eat no bread and drink no water," your corpse shall not come to the tomb of your fathers.' " So it was, after he had eaten bread and after he had drunk, that he saddled the donkey for him, the prophet whom he had brought back. When he was gone, a lion met him on the road and killed him. And his corpse was thrown on the road, and the donkey stood by it. The lion also stood by the corpse. And there, men passed by and saw the corpse thrown on the road, and the lion standing by the corpse. Then they went and told it in the city where the old prophet dwelt. Now when the prophet who had brought him back from the way heard it, he said, "It is the man of God who was disobedient to the word of the LORD. Therefore the LORD has delivered him to the lion, which has torn him and killed him, according to the word of the LORD which He spoke to him." And he spoke to his sons, saying, "Saddle the donkey for me." So they saddled it. Then he went and found his corpse thrown on the road, and the donkey and the lion standing by the corpse. The lion had not eaten the corpse nor torn the donkey. And the prophet took up the corpse of the man of God, laid it on the donkey, and brought it back. So the old prophet came to the city to mourn, and to bury him. Then he laid the corpse in his own tomb; and they mourned over him, saying, "Alas, my brother!" So it was, after he had buried him, that he spoke to his sons, saying, "When I am dead, then bury me in the tomb where the man of God is buried; lay my bones beside his bones. For the saying which he cried out by the word of the LORD against the altar in Bethel, and against all the shrines on the high places which are in the cities of Samaria, will surely come to pass." After this event Jeroboam did not turn from his evil way, but again he made priests from every class of people for the high places; whoever wished, he consecrated him, and he became one of the priests of the high places. And this thing was the sin of the house of Jeroboam, so as to exterminate and destroy it from the face of the earth. —1 Kings 13:11-34

DON'T TRY TO CONTROL OR MANIPULATE SOMEONE'S ACTIONS USING PERSONAL PROPHECY

Now it came to pass, that when we had departed from them and set sail, running a straight course we came to Cos, the following day to Rhodes, and from there to Patara. And finding a ship sailing over to Phoenicia, we went aboard and set sail. When we had sighted Cyprus, we passed it on the left, sailed to Syria, and landed at Tyre; for there the ship was to unload her cargo. And finding disciples, we stayed there seven days. They told Paul through the Spirit not to go up to Jerusalem. When we had come to the end of those days, we departed and went on our way; and they all accompanied us, with wives and children, till we were out of the city. And we knelt down on the shore and prayed. When we had taken our leave of one another, we boarded the ship, and they returned home. And when we had finished our voyage from Tyre, we came to Ptolemais, greeted the brethren, and stayed with them one day. On the next day we who were Paul's companions departed and came to Caesarea, and entered the house of Philip the evangelist, who was one of the seven, and stayed with him. Now this man had four virgin daughters who prophesied. <u>And as we stayed many days, a certain prophet named Agabus came down from Judea. When he had come to us, he took Paul's belt, bound his own hands and feet, and said, "Thus says the Holy Spirit, 'So shall the Jews at Jerusalem bind the man who owns this belt, and deliver him into the hands of the Gentiles.' " Now when we heard these things, both we and those from that place pleaded with him not to go up to Jerusalem. Then Paul answered, "What do you mean by weeping and breaking my heart? For I am ready not only to be bound, but also to die at Jerusalem for the name of the Lord Jesus."</u> So when he would not be persuaded, we ceased, saying, "The will of the Lord be done." And after those days we packed and went up to Jerusalem. Also some of the disciples from Caesarea went with us and brought with them a certain Mnason of Cyprus, an early disciple, with whom we were to lodge.—Acts 21:1-16

Reflections, Reviews, Questions

40. How do you judge the prophetic words?

_____

_____

_____

41. What are the tell tell signs that the prophetic word source is not of the Lord?

_____

_____

_____

42. Is control and manipulation associated with witchcraft?

_____

_____

_____

43. What have you learned about performing the last word the Lord has given you as instructions and not be swayed by people who pretend they heard from God for you?

_____

_____

_____

Notes

_____

_____

_____

_____

_____

_____

_____

_____

_____

Discerning the Source

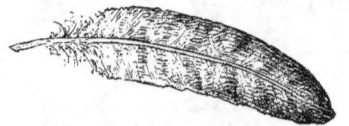

*And it came to pass, as we went to prayer, a certain **damsel possessed with a spirit of divination** met us, which brought her masters much gain by <u>soothsaying</u>: —17 The same followed Paul and us, and <u>cried, saying</u>, **These men are the servants of the most high God, which shew unto us the way of salvation.** —18 <u>And this did she many days</u>. But Paul, <u>being grieved, turned and said to the spirit, I command thee in the name of Jesus Christ to come out of her.</u> And he came out the same hour. —Acts 16:16-18*

CATEGORIES USED TO TEST PROPHECY

The source:

a. **God (The Kingdom of Light)**
    o   The Father
    o   The Son
    o   Holy Spirit
    o   Good Principalities, Good Powers, Good Rulers,
    o   Angels, Heavenly Creatures, Perfected Saints in the heavenly places

b. **Flesh**
    o   Carnal Mind (Soul)
    o   Hidden Desires of the flesh
    o   Lust of the flesh, Lust of the eyes and the Pride of Life

c. **Evil Spirits (The kingdom of darkness)**
    o   Satan
    o   Fallen Angels
    o   Evil Principalities, Evil Powers, and Evil Rulers
    o   Devils, Demons, and Familiar spirits

SPIRITUAL DISCERNMENT

But the natural man receiveth not the things of the Spirit of God: for they are foolishness unto him: neither can he know them, because they are spiritually discerned. —1 Corinthians 2:14

Thayer[9] Definition: ἀνακρίνω | anakrinō is to examine or judge, to investigate, examine, enquire into, scrutinize, sift, question. It is also to judge off, estimate, determine (the excellence or defects of any person or thing

JUDGING PROPHECY

Does the prophecy glorify Jesus, the speaker, or you?

In order for us to truly judge prophecy aside from the fragrance of Jesus on the prophetic word, we must learn to ask these important questions. These questions will help you get an overall picture of the word. The motives and character of those involved or delivering the prophecy will be revealed. It is important to always take into account the character and track record of those delivering prophetic messages. Ultimately, everything has an impact.

- o Does the prophetic word align with the Word of God?
- o Is the person delivering the prophetic message a follower of Jesus?
- o Is there evidence of a proven track record in their character?
- o Is the way the message is being delivered understandable to you?
- o Does it flow with what's happening or was it out of order?
- o Did you experience a sense of peace when someone prophesied to you?
- o Do I feel comforted, uplifted, or cheered up?
- o What's your response to that?
- o Was it confirming?

---

[9] Thayer, *Thayer's Greek-English Lexicon of the New Testament.*

Reflections, Reviews, Questions

44. What are the three categories or sources of voices?

_____

_____

_____

_____

45. What is the Thayer definition of examine or judge?

_____

_____

_____

_____

46. While judging the prophetic word what are some of the questions you should be asking?

_____

_____

_____

_____

Notes

_____

_____

_____

_____

_____

Prophetic Teams

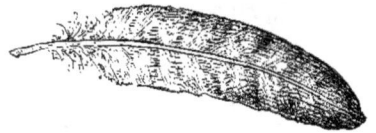

Prophetic Teams/Presbytery/Ministry (elders or council of leaders)

*For **you can all prophesy** one by one, that all may learn and all may be encouraged.—1 Corinthians 14:31*

- o   One by one (in an orderly fashion)
- o   For learning and impartation
- o   For encouragement and building of the body

According to 1 Corinthians 14:31, the safest and most effective way to learn and grow in the gift of prophecy is by prophesying in teams and seeking the guidance of multiple counselors. I have observed that when individuals collaborate in teams, there is a noticeable increase in trust and flexibility when it comes to sharing prophetic insights. To put it differently, when you are part of a team consisting of individuals who share similar prophetic beliefs, it becomes effortless to express prophetic words. The synergy created when prophets assemble seems to generate a profound vortex of prophetic inspiration. When one person delivers a prophecy, the rest of the group listens and gains knowledge.

Where no counsel is, the people fall: but in the multitude of counsellors there is safety. —Proverbs 11:14
And the spirits of the prophets are subject to the prophets. —1 Corinthians 14:32

Prophets and those with prophetic gifts must acknowledge the multidimensional nature of the phrase "the spirit of the prophets is subject to the prophet," which encompasses a variety of ideas. For the moment in the context of prophetic teams, I want you to focus on this. You are more power in a prophetic company then when you are alone. It seems as though you are collectively joining anointing into one big pot and everyone is in turn using the same pot with everyone's supplies.

From whom the whole body fitly joined together and compacted by that which every joint supplieth, according to the effectual working in the measure of every part, maketh increase of the body unto the edifying of itself in love. —Ephesians 4:16

According to numerous scriptures, the non-prophetic individuals who join a group of prophets are seen to have the prophetic anointing spontaneously manifest within them. We have learned in the School of the Prophets that this is the most effective way to grow and exercise by "reason of use" the prophetic gift, it is to work in teams. There is a tangible impartation and synergistic effect the more regularly this is done through activations. Learn and grow together.

Reflections, Reviews, Questions

47. Why are Prophetic Teams so important and necessary in a church or community?

_____

_____

48. Why is it important to encourage the body via prophecy and using teams to do so?

_____

_____

49. Why is it important to prophesy one by one and in an orderly fashion?

_____

_____

50. How do you learn to prophesy when you are prophesying in teams, rather than if you were prophesying as a lone ranger?

_____

_____

51. Why should prophetic teams consist of elders or presbytery leaders?

_____

_____

Notes

_____

_____

_____

_____

_____

_____

_____

_____

Keys to hearing God's voice through scribing

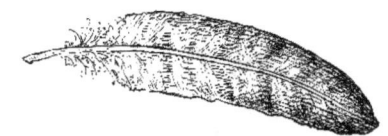

I will <u>stand my watch</u> And <u>set myself on the rampart</u>, And <u>watch to see</u> what <u>He will say to me</u>, And what I will answer when I am corrected. Then the LORD answered me and said: "<u>Write the vision</u> And <u>make it plain on tablets</u>, That he may run who reads it. For the vision is yet for an appointed time; But at the end it will speak, and it will not lie. Though it tarries, wait for it; Because it will surely come, It will not tarry. "Behold the proud, His soul is not upright in him; But the just shall live by his faith. —Habakkuk 2:1-4

My tongue is <u>the pen of a ready writer.</u> —Psalms 45:1c

<u>And the LORD said unto Moses, Write</u> this for a memorial in a book, and rehearse it in the ears of Joshua: for I will utterly put out the remembrance of Amalek from under heaven. —Exodus 17:14

Moreover the LORD said unto me, Take thee a great roll, and write in it with a man's pen concerning Mahershalalhashbaz. —Isaiah 8:1

In order to flow in the Seer flow and begin to sense God through our five natural senses and write, the first necessary ingredient is tranquility. When it comes to meditation, there exists a wide range of techniques that can be practiced in the presence of the Lord. One effective method involves utilizing the Word of God as a tool for calibration during moments of rest following a worship session in the divine presence of the Lord. The type of centering prayer I am referring to is one that enables you to come before the Lord without any specific agendas or requests, but rather to fully embrace His presence and His will for your life. This is called contemplative prayer or listening prayer. Today we often call it soaking prayers. Refer to School of the Holy Spirit Manual 4 "Praying, Waiting, Listening, Walking and Ascending".

During the next phase of contemplative prayer, our focus shifts towards learning to see and understand what God is revealing to us. By examining the teachings of the Habakkuk 2 scripture, we can gain insight into the importance of standing watch and being open to what He will reveal to us. The sole moment when we are able to perceive our own reflections on the surface of a lake is when it remains completely calm and undisturbed. The formation of visions typically initiates with still images, gradually transitioning into fully animated, dynamic motion pictures.

It is after an ecstatic moments in the visions and insights of God that we awaken and begin to write. In this kind of relax state our hand and our tongue become the pen of a ready writer. The flow of words from our spirit finds its direct conduit to the pages before us. True Journaling goes beyond simply taking responsibility for the revelations that the Lord imparts in the spiritual realm; it also involves capturing a moment that transcends the boundaries of time and space. These words and accounts that we have personally encountered allow us to continuously revisit these timeless experiences when we read them. These are the benefits of journaling spiritual experiences.

Journaling or scribing is a powerful way to hear and capturing the heart of the Father. The gift will increase by reason of use.

1) In order to eliminate both external and internal distractions, engage in self-deliverance sessions.

2) Calibrate yourself on the word of God, such as reading Psalm 119 in it's entirety. Then Quiet your thoughts by chewing on the Word of the Lord.

3) Ask Holy Spirit to come and to fill you with His Presence and Love as you ponder on His goodness.

4) Write down the flow of thoughts and pictures that come to you with no agenda of sounding deep, just write.

BY REVELATION

*Now, brethren, if I come unto you speaking with tongues, what shall I profit you, except I shall speak to you either **by revelation**, or by knowledge, or by prophesying, or by doctrine?*
—1 Corinthians 14:6

When Jesus came into the coasts of Caesarea Philippi, he asked his disciples, saying, Whom do men say that I the Son of man am? —14 And they said, Some say that thou art John the Baptist: some, Elias; and others, Jeremias, or one of the prophets. —15 He saith unto them, But whom say ye that I am? —16 And Simon Peter answered and said, Thou art the Christ, the Son of the living God. —17 And Jesus answered and said unto him, Blessed art thou, Simon Barjona: for flesh and blood hath not revealed it unto thee, but my Father which is in heaven. —18 And I say also unto thee, That thou art Peter, and upon this rock I will build my church; and the gates of hell shall not prevail against it. —19 And I will give unto thee the keys of the kingdom of heaven: and whatsoever thou shalt bind on earth shall be bound in heaven: and whatsoever thou shalt loose on earth shall be loosed in heaven. —20 Then charged he his disciples that they should tell no man that he was Jesus the Christ. —Matthew 16:13-20

In order to be recognized as the best writers of our time, it is essential for writers to go beyond mere research, study, and personal experiences, and tap into a profound connection with the Father, from whom they receive divine revelation. By witnessing the Father's activities in the heavenly realms, they gain insight and then translate it into action here on earth. By revealing the heavenly patterns, they provide us with a blueprint to follow, which in turn brings the will of God onto the earth. The rock or process that effectively builds the church of God is the process of receiving revelation from the Father and bringing it to the hearts of men, and nothing has the power to hinder it.

Reflections, Reviews, Questions

52. List the four steps to get to a place of scribing or journaling?

_____

_____

_____

53. What does it mean to Calibrate oneself when reading Psalm 119?

_____

_____

_____

54. What is the "rock" or "process" by which Jesus said the Church will be built upon?

_____

_____

_____

55. If you were to speak to people in tongues they may not understand you unless the Lord gives them an interpretation. So, what are the best way to speak to people so that they can profit or benefit?

_____

_____

_____

56. Why is it important and advantageous to write or journal your revelation?

_____

_____

_____

Notes

_____

_____

_____

_____

_____

Seers and Prophets

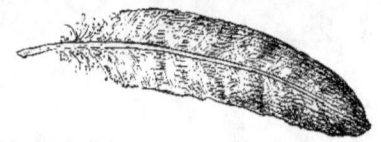

Similar to the Nile River, which originates from one source, then develops into multiple streams.[10]

1. **In the Hebrew language, the term "Nabiy" is used to refer to a prophet.** (Jeremiah 1:5,9, Deuteronomy 18:18, Exodus 7:1, Exodus 4:15-16.)

   Before I formed thee in the belly, I knew thee; and before thou camest forth out of the womb I sanctified thee, and I ordained thee a prophet unto the nations. —Jeremiah 1:5

   Then the LORD put forth his hand, and touched my mouth. And the LORD said unto me, Behold, I have put my words in thy mouth. —Jeremiah 1:9

   I will raise them up a Prophet from among their brethren, like unto thee, and will put my words in his mouth; and he shall speak unto them all that I shall command him. —Deuteronomy 18:18

   And thou shalt speak unto him, and put words in his mouth: and I will be with thy mouth, and with his mouth, and will teach you what ye shall do. And he shall be thy spokesman unto the people: and he shall be, even he shall be to thee instead of a mouth, and thou shalt be to him instead of God. —Exodus 4:15-16

   And the LORD said unto Moses, See, I have made thee a god to Pharaoh: and Aaron thy brother shall be thy prophet. —Exodus 7:1

2. **"Ro'eh," "Ra'ah," and "Chozeh" are different variations of the Hebrew word that translates to "seer."** (1 Samuel 9:9 – Samuel, 2 Samuel 24:11—Gad, 2 Samuel 7:2 –Nathan, 2 Chronicles 29:30 –Asaph.)

   That the king said unto Nathan the prophet, See now, I dwell in an house of cedar, but the ark of God dwelleth within curtains. —2 Samuel 7:2

   (Beforetime in Israel, when a man went to enquire of God, thus he spake, Come, and let us go to the seer: for he that is now called a Prophet was beforetime called a Seer.) —1 Samuel 9:9

   For when David was up in the morning, the word of the LORD came unto the prophet Gad, David's seer, saying, —2 Samuel 24:11

---

[10] James W. Goll and Mark Chironna, *The Seer Expanded Edition: The Prophetic Power of Visions, Dreams and Open Heavens*, Expanded edition (Shippensburg, PA: Destiny Image Publishers, 2012).

Moreover, Hezekiah the king and the princes commanded the Levites to sing praise unto the LORD with the words of David, and of Asaph the seer. And they sang praises with gladness, and they bowed their heads and worshipped. —2 Chronicles 29:30

The topic of the seer necessitates an examination of both pre-cross prophets and post-cross prophets. According to my understanding, Jesus, upon His ascension, granted "doma" gifts to mankind specifically for the purpose of ministry work and to equip the saints. Furthermore, it is my belief that these gifts were restricted to five specific roles, namely apostles, prophets, evangelists, pastors, and teachers, as stated in Ephesian 4:11. "And he gave some, apostles; and some, prophets; and some, evangelists; and some, pastors and teachers. I am only able to count up to five, not six. The prophet is a whole entity and is not divided into two parts. In spite of that, in the old testament, they were called by varying names. These varying names based on their functions depicted specifically in Isaiah 29:10 which states, "For the LORD has poured out on you The spirit of deep sleep, And has closed your eyes, namely, the prophets; And He has covered your heads, namely, the seers." Seers not only could see like prophets, but use their entire heads to sense the Word of the Lord. The Prophets, referred to as Nabiys, had their perception confined to their spiritual sight exclusively. This is the reason why some individuals argue that "every Seer is capable of functioning as a Prophet, but a Prophet is incapable of functioning as a Seer.I believe this statement holds true solely within the context of the Old Testament, with limitations imposed by the pre-cross era. I am of the belief that Jesus has brought about a change in that matter. Those limitations have been removed, granting us access to both the left and right hand of the prophetic flows. This is the rationale behind my choice to label them as prophetic flows and styles, distinguishing them from the prophetic offices mentioned in the old testament. It can be observed that neither Jesus nor Paul made any assertions regarding the distinction between Seers and Nabiys in the New Testament. It is my understanding that the New Testament prophets are unified as one. I am a firm believer in the existence of prophets who possess two hands. It is not uncommon for individuals to have one hand that is more dominant than the other. This we would consider the active or more prevalent manifestation of either the seer flow or the nabiy flow. Just like those who were born left hand dominant could train to use their weak right hand, so in the spiritual realm we can exercise both types of flows or styles. One of my friends, Jeff Jansen, who has since passed away and gone to be with the Lord, once prophesied about the emergence of ambidextrous prophets. I strongly hold the belief that the prevalence of this phenomenon is not solely attributed to cross pollination in the streams, but it is also driven by the divine purpose of God on earth. Jesus gives us access to a new man, Christ Jesus, who is the hope of Glory in each and every one of us. To obtain additional information, please refer to my teachings on the Nabiy and Seer Flow, accessible on YouTube.

Reflections, Reviews, Questions

57. Does the author of this manual believe that seers and prophets in the New Testament are two separate entities or one? Why does He refer to these has prophetic styles and flows instead of offices in reference to their New Testament functions?

_____

_____

_____

58. Which hand in the spiritual realm do you believe is your strong hand and if you don't have a dominant hand are you ambidextrous?

_____

_____

_____

59. In addition, the author of this manual expresses the viewpoint that New Testament Prophets exhibit traits of both seers and prophets (nabiy flow), and he offers an illustration of how he interprets the symbolism of the left hand and right hand. Could you share an example from the text?

_____

_____

_____

60. According to the authors supplementary teaching what is the difference between the nabiy flow and the seer flow?

_____

_____

_____

61. How do you access the nabiy flow verses accessing the seer flow?

_____

_____

_____

62. Give one scripture found in the Old Testament which shows the effects of God's judgment from deep sleep on both seers and prophets and what else can you deduct from that scripture?

_____
_____
_____

Notes

_____
_____
_____
_____
_____
_____
_____
_____
_____

Prophetic Flows

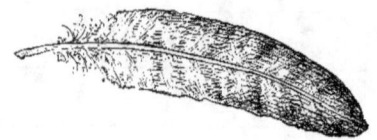

- o **Nabiy (Prophet):** the flowing forth, or the bubble forth like the fountain, to let drop, to lift up, or to spring forth.
- o **Seer (Rohe, Raha):** stillness and flow or revelation by all senses including visions with great detail
- o **Revelatory or Propheteia (Greek):** speaking forth the mind and the counsel of God, or to speak for another.
- o **Ecstatic Prophecy:** ecstatic visions, trances, and supernatural experiences such as biblical translations, transportations, transfigurations, translocations, and biblical levitations (Enoch, Elijah, (1 Kings 18:12, 2 Kings 2:1, 11), The Messenger in Revelation 19:10b, Ezekiel in Ezekiel 8:3, Philip Acts 8:39).

And it shall come to pass, as soon as I am gone from thee, that the Spirit of the LORD shall carry thee whither I know not; and so when I come and tell Ahab, and he cannot find thee, he shall slay me: but I thy servant fear the LORD from my youth. —1 Kings 18:12

And it came to pass, as they still went on, and talked, that, behold, there appeared a chariot of fire, and horses of fire, and parted them both asunder; and Elijah went up by a whirlwind into heaven. —2 Kings 2:11

And I fell at his feet to worship him. And he said unto me, See thou do it not: I am thy fellowservant, and of thy brethren that have the testimony of Jesus: worship God…—Revelation 19:10b

And when they were come up out of the water, the Spirit of the Lord caught away Philip, that the eunuch saw him no more: and he went on his way rejoicing. —Acts 8:39

And Enoch walked with God: and he was not; for God took him. —Genesis 5:24

- o **Massa (Burden):** the burden of the Lord, or when the hand of the Lord is upon you.
- o **Nataph:** to let it drop like rain.

And there ran a young man, and told Moses, and said, Eldad and Medad do prophesy in the camp. —Numbers 11:27

By considering applications and experience, we are able to classify our prophetic flows into these recognized categories. I don't believe we should limit them to only five. In my opinion, the naming conventions are not rigid and can differ depending on individual preference. Certain individuals may opt for the term "Revelatory Flow" as opposed to the utilization of the Greek term "Propheteia." Most of these are found as Hebrew words in the bible that were used in the translations for the word "Prophecy."

Reflections, Reviews, Questions

63. What are the other prophetic flows mentioned other than the nabiy and seer flow that we have discovered so far?

_____

_____

_____

64. Which of the flows do you believe is your strongest flow and do you believe you have experienced all of them?

_____

_____

_____

Notes

_____

_____

_____

_____

_____

_____

_____

_____

_____

The Ways God Communicates with His people

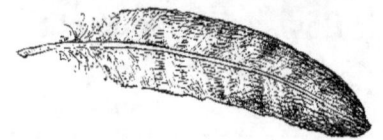

*And Miriam and Aaron spake against Moses because of the Ethiopian woman whom he had married: for he had married an Ethiopian woman. —2 And they said, Hath the LORD indeed spoken only by Moses? hath he not spoken also by us? And the LORD heard it. —3 (Now the man **Moses was very meek, above all the men which were upon the face of the earth**.) —4 And the LORD spake suddenly unto Moses, and unto Aaron, and unto Miriam, Come out ye three unto the tabernacle of the congregation. And they three came out. —5 **And the LORD came down in the pillar of the cloud, and stood in the door of the tabernacle,** and called Aaron and Miriam: and they both came forth. —6 And he said, Hear now my words: **If there be a prophet among you, I the LORD will make myself known unto him in a <u>vision</u>,** and **will speak unto him in <u>a dream.</u>** —7 My servant Moses is not so, who is faithful in all mine house. —8 With him will **I speak mouth to mouth, even apparently**, and **not in <u>dark speeches</u>;** and **the similitude of the LORD shall he behold**: wherefore then were ye not afraid to speak against my servant Moses? — Numbers 12:1-8*

FIVE MAJOR CATEGORIES OF COMMUNICATION[11]

1. **Dreams and visions have the ability to transcend language barriers, allowing for a universal understanding.**

2. **Vision:**
   - a). When in a trance, the mind is almost entirely suspended.
   - b). Pictures/Imaginations: flashing through our Imaginations
   - c). Our eyes serve as a gateway, allowing us to see into the mystical and spiritual dimensions. Having the ability to see in the spirit realm.

3. **"Dark Speech" is an intriguing subject that warrants exploration, especially when considering its utilization of figurative language and the profound impressions it evokes.** Through the use of puns, parables, riddles, and signs, God communicates in a mysterious manner known as dark speech. Proverbs 1:6, 1 Kings 10:1

4. **The direct inner audible voice refers to the ability to hear within our spirit and outside of our mind.**

---

[11] John Sandford and Paula Sandford, *The Elijah Task: A Call to Today's Prophets and Intercessors*, Annotated edition (Lake Mary, Fla: Charisma House, 2006).

5. Audible: **In a way that can be heard by everyone: In a voice loud enough for everyone to hear.**
The events of Numbers 12, and the Mount of Transfiguration, as described in Matthew 17:5 and also the Baptism of Jesus are accounts that should be studied further.

See also John 12:28 Paul on the road to Damascus.

See also (Matthew 3:17 NKJV) And suddenly a voice came from heaven, saying, "This is My beloved Son, in whom I am well pleased."

When it comes to the Prophetic, there are a few levels of representations that are frequently seen.

- The Spirit of Prophecy (Revelation 19:10)
- Prophetic Teams (presbytery or elders)
- The Gift of Prophecy (1 Corinthians 13:2, 1 Cor 12:10)
- The Office of the New Testament Prophet
- Round Table of Prophets
- Prophetic Cultures
- Prophetic Musicians and Bands
- Prophetic Counsels of Elders or Networks

Worship God: for the testimony of Jesus is the spirit of prophecy. —Revelation 19:10c

And though I have the gift of prophecy, and understand all mysteries, and all knowledge; and though I have all faith, so that I could remove mountains, and have not charity, I am nothing. —1 Corinthians 13:2

To another the working of miracles; to another prophecy; to another discerning of spirits; to another diverse kinds of tongues; to another the interpretation of tongues: —1 Corinthians 12:10

The Prophet or Nabiy Style: usually builds up with the most holy faith of exercising tongues and interpretation of tongues in order to tune into the prophetic flow. There is a river on which the teams or the prophetic people will spontaneously catch, step into the presence and inspiration of the Holy Spirit. This style can be initiated at any time. It is most effective when used in conjunction with the Massa or burden of the Lord in a worship service or when the Lord comes upon an individual or people.

The Seer Style—Ro'eh (Ra'ah): Although, it appears that this occurs with more preparation and focuses more on visions and seeing in the spirit realms. This style is in conjunction with the Nataph to where each word is crafted and contemplated on. Those who use this style the most step into a scribal style anointing via journaling the thoughts of the Lord as their conscience are bearing witness. This Style works best for prophetic round tables, correction, directions, and warnings. Those who usually use this style see more pictures and visions and interpret dreams on paper.

There is a reason I don't call these separate and independent prophetic offices. It is my belief based on my interpretation of scripture that the Lord Jesus brought the union of all the prophetic offices into one New Testament prophetic office. Although there are many people who can choose to lean on one more than another naturally, it does not limit them to one flavor in the prophetic. Just like in some cultures, people may be required to use only their right hand for eating or shaking hands, prohibiting the use of the left hand. They forced some of these people, who were born either ambidextrous or left-handed, to use their right hand for writing, eating, and shaking hands. I believe that through proper training, we can teach those who are naturally left-handed to use their right hand. Hence, in the prophetic we all have access to prophesy in the Nabiy Style and the Seer Style, because in Jesus we have access to both.

Reflections, Reviews, Questions

65. What are the five known major categories based on Numbers 12 that God generally communicates with the prophets?

_____

_____

_____

_____

66. What are the levels of expressions in the prophetic?

_____

_____

_____

Notes

_____

_____

_____

_____

_____

_____

_____

_____

_____

The way we receive a prophetic word

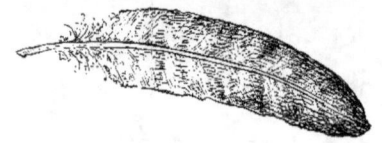

1. REVELATION

Sources of Revelation:

a) The Holy Spirit (The Spirit of God)

For the prophecy came not in old time by the will of man: but holy men of God spake as they were moved by the Holy Ghost. —2 Peter 1:21

The Spirit of Truth

The Angelic messengers.

b) The Human self (the flesh, carnal mind, or soulish)

And the word of the LORD came unto me, saying, —2 Son of man, prophesy against the prophets of Israel that prophesy, and say thou unto them that prophesy out of their own hearts, Hear ye the word of the LORD; —3 Thus saith the Lord GOD; Woe unto the foolish prophets, that follow their own spirit, and have seen nothing! —4 O Israel, thy prophets are like the foxes in the deserts. —5 Ye have not gone up into the gaps, neither made up the hedge for the house of Israel to stand in the battle in the day of the LORD. —6 They have seen vanity and lying divination, saying, The LORD saith: and the LORD hath not sent them: and they have made others to hope that they would confirm the word. —7 Have ye not seen a vain vision, and have ye not spoken a lying divination, whereas ye say, The LORD saith it; albeit I have not spoken? —8 Therefore thus saith the Lord GOD; Because ye have spoken vanity, and seen lies, therefore, behold, I am against you, saith the Lord GOD. —9 And mine hand shall be upon the prophets that see vanity, and that divine lies: they shall not be in the assembly of my people, neither shall they be written in the writing of the house of Israel, neither shall they enter into the land of Israel; and ye shall know that I am the Lord GOD. —10 Because, even because they have seduced my people, saying, Peace; and there was no peace; and one built up a wall, and, lo, others daubed it with untempered morter: —11 Say unto them which daub it with untempered morter, that it shall fall: there shall be an overflowing shower; and ye, O great hailstones, shall fall; and a stormy wind shall rend it. —12 Lo, when the wall is fallen, shall it not be said unto you, Where is the daubing wherewith ye have daubed it? —13 Therefore thus saith the Lord GOD; I will even rend it with a stormy wind in my fury; and there shall be an overflowing shower in mine anger, and great hailstones in my fury to consume it. —Ezekiel 13:1-7

Thus saith the LORD of hosts, Hearken not unto the words of the prophets that prophesy unto you: they make you vain: they speak a vision of their own heart, and not out of the mouth of the LORD. —17 They say still unto them that despise me, The LORD hath said, Ye shall have peace; and they say unto every one that walketh after the imagination of his own heart, No evil shall come upon you. "—Jeremiah 23:16-17

c) **The Evil spirits** (lying spirit or the spirit of error)

And it came to pass, as we went to prayer, a certain damsel possessed with a spirit of divination met us, which brought her masters much gain by soothsaying: —17 The same followed Paul and us, and cried, saying, These men are the servants of the most high God, which shew unto us the way of salvation. —18 And this did she many days. But Paul, being grieved, turned and said to the spirit, I command thee in the name of Jesus Christ to come out of her. And he came out the same hour. —19 And when her masters saw that the hope of their gains was gone, they caught Paul and Silas, and drew them into the marketplace unto the rulers, —Acts 16:16-19

2. INTERPRETATION

Interpretation differs from translation. It's not a verbatim dictation from the Lord, but rather your interpretation of revelation's meaning.

When we get to interpretation of the revelation, this is where there is a separation from those who are mature and the novice.

We simply deliver some prophetic pictures and words the way they were received, without the need for interpretation.

Relying on Holy Spirit for what He means and says is the key to interpretation. Ask Holy Spirit what He is saying to the hearers.

But the Comforter, which is the Holy Ghost, whom the Father will send in my name, he shall teach you all things, and bring all things to your remembrance, whatsoever I have said unto you. —John 14:26

Interpret don't give an opinion.

In the multitude of words there wanteth not sin: but he that refraineth his lips is wise. —Proverbs 10:19

Being in a position of a clear conscience by removing all opinions, offenses, bitterness, sin, pride, and carnal perspectives

3. APPLICATION (DELIVERY AND TIMING)

Delivery and **Timing** is where the percentage of errors increases exponentially.

He who keeps his command will experience nothing harmful; And a wise man's heart discerns both time and judgment, Because for every matter there is a time and judgment, Though the misery of man increases greatly.—Ecclesiastes 8:5-6

_____

Don't go beyond your level of faith—stay humble.

_____

*Having then gifts differing according to the grace that is given to us, whether prophecy, **let us prophesy according to the proportion of faith;** —Romans 12:6*

Prophesy from the position of grace (we are under the era of grace and truth and not the law). The Lord Jesus has fulfilled the Law and the Prophets. Mercy triumphs over judgment.

Prophesy from the presence of the Lord.

Reflections, Reviews, Questions

67. What does the acronym RIA stand for?

_____

_____

_____

68. What are the two subcategories under the last acronym (A) in RIA?

_____

_____

_____

69. Out of the three RIA acronym, which of the three has the highest percentage of errors increasing exponentially?

_____

_____

_____

Notes

_____

_____

_____

_____

_____

_____

_____

_____

What are activations and are they Biblical?

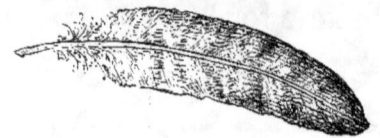

WHERE WE GET THE WORD "ACTIVATION"

This word "Activation" was coined by Bishop Bill Hamon, inspired by the following scripture.

> *Wherefore I put thee in remembrance that thou* **stir up** *the gift of God, which is in thee <u>by the putting on of my hands.</u>* —2 Timothy 1:6

The gifts are granted by the Lord, yet it's the believers' faith that activates them. The sovereign gifts are available to all individuals.

> *"The same way you believe in your heart and confess with your heart for salvation that Jesus is the Son of God, came into your heart, forgave you of your sins, and that he resurrected from the dead, is the same way you activate the gifts."* —Bill Hamon

---

You have activated the divine gift of salvation.

ἀναζωπυρέω | anazōpureō

According to Strong's Greek word anazōpureō is to Stir up is or to *re-enkindle*[12] :

Thayer Definition[13] : to kindle up, inflame one's zeal

The Miriam Webster[14] definition for Activation: the action or process of making something active or operative.

Likewise, in Chemistry: the process of making a substance chemically or *catalytically* active. Prophets catalyze!

> Let me *introduce you to several new words we use in our school. The first word is Calibration: It is what you do during an activation process in order to activate prophetically. For example, praying in tongues is a form of calibration prior to prophesying. Reading the Word of God and meditating on the Word of God is another calibration. You may also calibrate during an activation by singing a prophetic song of the Lord. Calibrations are spiritual techniques or technologies that helps you activate the prophetic gift. See page 102.*
>
> *Another Word in our prophetic culture in ours school is "Calisthenics." A Calisthenics is a prophetic stretch exercise that stretches you and strengthens your activations to another level or threshold or endurance level.*

---

[12] James Strong, *The New Strong's Expanded Exhaustive Concordance of the Bible*, Expanded edition (Thomas Nelson, 2010).

[13] Thayer, *Thayer's Greek-English Lexicon of the New Testament.*

[14] "Dictionary by Merriam-Webster: America's Most-Trusted Online Dictionary," accessed March 26, 2022, https://www.merriam-webster.com/.

Reflections, Reviews, Questions

70. What is a prophetic Activation? What is a prophetic Calibration? What is a prophetic Calisthenic exercise?

_____

_____

_____

_____

71. What scripture provided could you use in defense for activations?

_____

_____

_____

72. Who is a contemporary prophet of our generation who coined the word activation and paved the way for the prophetic?

_____

_____

_____

Notes

_____

_____

_____

_____

_____

_____

_____

_____

_____

Starting to Prophesy

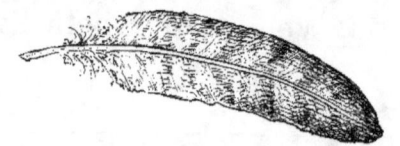

HAVE A REAL RELATIONSHIP WITH THE GIVER (HOLY SPIRIT)

Get the water and the wetness of the water will come.
Place the first commandment first.

But if from thence thou shalt seek the LORD thy God, thou shalt find him, if thou seek him with all thy heart and with all thy soul. —Deuteronomy 4:29

Hear, O Israel: The LORD our God is one LORD: And thou shalt love the LORD thy God with all thine heart, and with all thy soul, and with all thy might. And these words, which I command thee this day, shall be in thine heart: —Deuteronomy 6:4-6

Spend time in intimacy with the Lord for the sake of intimacy and not ministry.
After that then spend time with the Lord to prepare as a priest to minister to the Lord, before ministering to the people.

KNOW THAT YOU CAN PROPHESY AND REMAIN HUMBLE

Ye adulterers and adulteresses, know ye not that the friendship of the world is enmity with God? whosoever therefore will be a friend of the world is the enemy of God. —James 4:4

For thus saith the high and lofty One that inhabiteth eternity, whose name is Holy; I dwell in the high and holy place, with him also that is of a contrite and humble spirit, to revive the spirit of the humble, and to revive the heart of the contrite ones. —Isaiah 57:15

The LORD is nigh unto them that are of a broken heart; and saveth such as be of a contrite spirit. —Psalms 34:18

The sacrifices of God are a broken spirit: a broken and a contrite heart, O God, thou wilt not despise. —Psalms 51:17

Don't start with "thus says the Lord." Start with I feel the Lord is saying this or that.

"I prophesy just as I talk in tongues (by faith)." —Bill Hamon

Gift, grace, faith, in personal prophecy are the initial elements in the Nabi flow.

I will hear what God the LORD will speak: for he will speak peace unto his people, and to his saints: but let them not turn again to folly. —Psalms 85:8

For ye may all prophesy one by one, that all may learn, and all may be comforted. And the spirits of the prophets are subject to the prophets. For God is not the author of confusion, but of peace, as in all churches of the saints. —1 Corinthians 14:31-33

DESIRE (HUNGERING AND THIRSTING HIS RIGHTEOUSNESS)

Follow after charity, and desire spiritual gifts, but rather that ye may prophesy. —1 Corinthians 14:1

Wherefore, brethren, covet to prophesy, and forbid not to speak with tongues. —1 Corinthians 14:39

Read the Word and meditate on it day and night. The Word of God will be your gauge and foundation for prophesying biblically to others.

The expectation that the Lord will use you and you will hear from the Lord.

For who hath known the mind of the Lord, that he may instruct him? But we have the mind of Christ. — 1 Corinthians 2:16

PREPARATION AND PRACTICE MAKES PROFICIENT (TRAINING).

Do not neglect the gift that is in you, which was given to you by prophecy with the laying on of the hands of the eldership. —1 Timothy 4:14

Practice in the first person, by saying son or daughter. There seems to be a higher flow of anointing when you prophesy in the first person of the Holy Spirit in you.

Keep an active and consistent prayer life with daily reading of the Word.

Rejoice always, pray without ceasing, in everything give thanks; for this is the will of God in Christ Jesus for you. Do not quench the Spirit. Do not despise prophecies. Test all things; hold fast what is good. Abstain

from every form of evil. Now may the God of peace Himself sanctify you completely; and may your whole spirit, soul, and body be preserved blameless at the coming of our Lord Jesus Christ. He who calls you is faithful, who also will do it. Brethren, pray for us. Greet all the brethren with a holy kiss. I charge you by the Lord that this epistle be read to all the holy brethren. —1 Thessalonians 5:16-27 NKJV

Rejoice evermore. —17 Pray without ceasing. —18 In every thing give thanks: for this is the will of God in Christ Jesus concerning you. —19 Quench not the Spirit. —20 Despise not prophesyings. —21 Prove all things; hold fast that which is good. —22 Abstain from all appearance of evil. —23 And the very God of peace sanctify you wholly; and I pray God your whole spirit and soul and body be preserved blameless unto the coming of our Lord Jesus Christ. —24 Faithful is he that calleth you, who also will do it. —25 Brethren, pray for us. —26 Greet all the brethren with an holy kiss. —27 I charge you by the Lord that this epistle be read unto all the holy brethren.— 1 Thessalonians 5:16-27

Gifts are given to bless others, but fruits are grown (working them by practice, increases boldness and flow).

PRACTICE WITH ELDERS OR OTHER MATURE, EXPERIENCED ELDERS (PRESBYTERY) WHO HAVE PROPHESIED FOR YEARS.

Prophesy and practice in prophetic teams. Be accountable and responsible for your prophetic word. Keep track of your prophetic words and follow up. Learn self-control by not prophesying the first things that pop out of your mind.

*And beside this, giving all diligence, **add to your faith virtue**; and to virtue knowledge; —6 And to knowledge temperance; and to temperance patience; and to patience godliness; —7 And to godliness brotherly kindness; and to brotherly kindness charity. —8 For if these things be in you, and abound, they make you that ye shall neither be barren nor unfruitful in the knowledge of our Lord Jesus Christ. —9 But he that lacketh these things is blind, and cannot see afar off, and hath forgotten that he was purged from his old sins. —10 Wherefore the rather, brethren, give diligence to make your calling and election sure: for if ye do these things, ye shall never fall: —2 Peter 1:5-10*

MAKE YOUR MOTIVE LOVE AND ADD KNOWLEDGE, VIRTUE, AND DISCIPLINE TO YOUR PROPHETIC LIFESTYLE.

You can sharpen your target, accuracy, and acuteness with proper training in hearing the voice of God from those who have gone before you. Invest in books and recordings of others who have shown themselves to be reliable prophetic voices.

But wilt thou know, O vain man, that faith without works is dead? —James 2:20

*For every one that useth milk is unskilful in the word of righteousness: for he is a babe. But strong meat belongeth to them that are of full age, even those who **by reason of use** have their senses exercised to discern both good and evil. —Hebrews 5:13-14*

FASTING, PRAYER, AND TONGUES KEEP YOU PREPARED

A prayer lifestyle is a requirement to keep your flow.

An active prayer life which also can include meditative prayers and waiting before the Lord in silence.

Praying in tongues more and more...

I thank my God I speak with tongues more than you all;—1 Corinthians 14:18

WATCH AND SEE

I will <u>stand upon my watch</u>, and set me upon the tower, and <u>will watch to see what he will say unto me</u>, and what I shall answer when I am reproved. —Habakkuk 2:1

And the LORD answered me, and said, <u>Write the vision</u>, and <u>make it plain upon tables</u>, that <u>he may run that readeth it</u>. —3 For the vision is yet for an appointed time, but at the end it shall speak, and not lie: though it tarry, wait for it; because it will surely come, it will not tarry. —4 Behold, his soul which is lifted up is not upright in him: but the just shall live by his faith. —Habakkuk 2:2-4

The words of Jeremiah the son of Hilkiah, of the priests who were in Anathoth in the land of Benjamin, —2 to whom the word of the LORD came in the days of Josiah the son of Amon, king of Judah, in the thirteenth year of his reign. —3 It came also in the days of Jehoiakim the son of Josiah, king of Judah, until the end of the eleventh year of Zedekiah the son of Josiah, king of Judah, until the carrying away of Jerusalem captive in the fifth month. —4 Then the word of the LORD came to me, saying: —5 "Before I formed you in the womb I knew you; Before you were born I sanctified you; I ordained you a prophet to the nations." —6 Then said I: "Ah, Lord GOD! Behold, I cannot speak, for I am a youth." —7 But the LORD said to me: "Do not say, 'I am a youth,' For you shall go to all to whom I send you, And whatever I command you, you shall speak. —8 Do not be afraid of their faces, For I am with you to deliver you," says the LORD. —9 Then the LORD put forth His hand and touched my mouth, and the LORD said to me: "Behold, I have put My words in your mouth. —10 See, I have this day set you over the nations and over the kingdoms, To root out and to pull down, To destroy and to throw down, To build and to plant." —11 Moreover the word of the LORD came to me, saying, "Jeremiah, what do you see?" And I said, "I see a branch of an almond tree." —12 Then the LORD said to me, "You have seen well, for I am ready to perform

My word." —13 And the word of the LORD came to me the second time, saying, "What do you see?" And I said, "I see a boiling pot, and it is facing away from the north." —14 Then the LORD said to me: "Out of the north calamity shall break forth On all the inhabitants of the land. —15 For behold, I am calling All the families of the kingdoms of the north," says the LORD; "They shall come and each one set his throne At the entrance of the gates of Jerusalem, Against all its walls all around, And against all the cities of Judah. —16 I will utter My judgments Against them concerning all their wickedness, Because they have forsaken Me, Burned incense to other gods, And worshiped the works of their own hands. —17 "Therefore prepare yourself and arise, And speak to them all that I command you. Do not be dismayed before their faces, Lest I dismay you before them. —18 For behold, I have made you this day A fortified city and an iron pillar, And bronze walls against the whole land—Against the kings of Judah, Against its princes, Against its priests, And against the people of the land. —19 They will fight against you, But they shall not prevail against you. For I am with you," says the LORD, "to deliver you." —Jeremiah 1:1-19

*The word that Isaiah the son of Amoz **saw** <u>concerning Judah and Jerusalem.</u> —2 And it shall come to pass in the last days, that the mountain of the LORD'S house shall be established in the top of the mountains, and shall be exalted above the hills; and all nations shall flow unto it. —3 And many people shall go and say, Come ye, and let us go up to the mountain of the LORD, to the house of the God of Jacob; and he will teach us of his ways, and we will walk in his paths: for out of Zion shall go forth the law, and the word of the LORD from Jerusalem. —Isaiah 2:1-3*

LOOK IN THE EYES

The same heard Paul speak: who stedfastly beholding him, and perceiving that he had faith to be healed, —Acts 14:9

Said with a loud voice, Stand upright on thy feet. And he leaped and walked. —Acts 14:10

THE DRIP OF THE PROPHETIC THAT FILLS TO OVERFLOW

SOMETIMES YOU WILL GET ONE PIECE AND THEN ONCE YOU RELEASE IT, YOU WILL GET MORE.

And the LORD said unto Samuel, How long wilt thou mourn for Saul, seeing I have rejected him from reigning over Israel? fill thine horn with oil, and go, I will send thee to Jesse the Bethlehemite: for I have provided me a king among his sons. —2 And Samuel said, How can I go? if Saul hear it, he will kill me. And the LORD said, Take an heifer with thee, and say, I am come to sacrifice to the LORD. —3 And call Jesse to the sacrifice, and I will shew thee what thou shalt do: and thou shalt anoint unto me him whom I name unto thee. —4 And Samuel did that which the LORD spake, and came to Bethlehem. And the elders of the town trembled at his coming, and said, Comest thou peaceably? —5 And he said, Peaceably: I am come to sacrifice unto the LORD: sanctify yourselves, and come with me to the sacrifice. And he sanctified Jesse and his sons, and called them to the sacrifice. —6 And it came to pass, when they were come, that he looked on Eliab, and said, Surely the LORD'S anointed is before him. —7 But the LORD said unto Samuel, Look not on his countenance, or on the height of his stature; because I have refused him: for the LORD seeth not as man seeth; for man looketh on the outward appearance, but the LORD looketh on the heart. —8 Then Jesse called Abinadab, and made him pass before Samuel. And he said, Neither hath the LORD chosen this. —9 Then Jesse made Shammah to pass by. And he said, Neither hath the LORD chosen this. —10 Again, Jesse made seven of his sons to pass before Samuel. And Samuel said unto Jesse, The LORD hath not chosen these. —11 And Samuel said unto Jesse, Are here all thy children? And he said, There remaineth yet the youngest, and, behold, he keepeth the sheep. And Samuel said unto Jesse, Send and fetch him: for we will not sit down till he come hither. —12 And he sent, and brought him in. Now he was ruddy, and withal of a beautiful countenance, and goodly to look to. And the LORD said, Arise, anoint him: for this is he. —13 Then Samuel took the horn of oil, and anointed him in the midst of his brethren: and the Spirit of the LORD came upon David from that day forward. So Samuel rose up, and went to Ramah. —1 Samuel 16:1-13

THE PROCESS OF THE FLOWING NABIY PROPHECY

1. Know that it's according to the Word (biblical understanding and scriptural)
2. Believe in your heart (make the Logos Rhema of God)

   That if thou <u>shalt confess with thy mouth</u> the Lord Jesus, and <u>shalt believe in thine heart</u> that <u>God hath raised him from the dead</u>, thou shalt be saved. For with the heart man believeth unto righteousness; and with the mouth confession is made unto salvation. —Romans 10:9-10

3. Confess with your mouth
4. Take actions (verbal action)

STICK TO THE BASICS INITIALLY

Comfort, Edification, Exhortation (all may prophesy)
Correction and Direction (should be left to those who are more mature in the prophetic in their ability to prophesy).
Stop rambling when you finish, don't counsel, and add and repeat yourself.

Let the prophets speak two or three, and <u>let the other judge.</u> —1 Corinthians 14:29

Know who to discern and judge prophetic words you receive.
If the word doesn't give you peace or isn't confirming place it on a shelf.

HOW YOU HEAR/SEE

INTUITION, PERCEPTION, IMPRESSIONS:

And said unto them, Sirs, I perceive that this voyage will be with hurt and much damage, not only of the lading and ship, but also of our lives. —Acts 27:10

And Jesus said, Who touched me? When all denied, Peter and they that were with him said, Master, the multitude throng thee and press thee, and sayest thou, Who touched me? And Jesus said, Somebody hath touched me: for I perceive that virtue is gone out of me. —Luke 8:45-46

Then Paul stood in the midst of Mars' hill, and said, Ye men of Athens, I perceive that in all things ye are too superstitious. —Acts 17:22

The woman saith unto him, Sir, I perceive that thou art a prophet. —John 4:19

Using your entire Spiritual Faculty will look like this:

- Dream, Visions, and Trances
- Nature, Stars, Sun and Moon, and the Cosmos
- The sudden and unexpected words that came out of his mouth were a spontaneous utterance.
- Mental Pictures
- Spiritual senses of sight, smell, test, touch, hearing, feel
- Body Checks
- Still small voice, Inner Voice and Bearing witness in your conscience:
- Audible Voice/Outer Audible
- Angels and Perfected Saints of Old
- Divine Appearances

New Testament Prophecy

- Prophecy is to be judged.
- Prophecy today is "in part."
- Prophecy is to be encouraged and practiced.
- Prophecy depends on the faith level of the one speaking.
- Prophecy often contains a conditional aspect. It's conditional when the condition is unexpressed.
- Stillness or quietness is important to be able to catch and press into the still small voice of the Lord or the impressions.

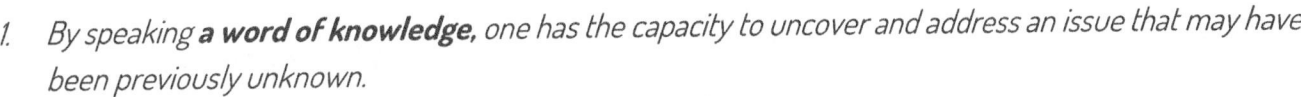

A WELL-BALANCED PROPHETIC WORD STRUCTURE:

1. By speaking **a word of knowledge,** one has the capacity to uncover and address an issue that may have been previously unknown.
2. The gift of **prophecy**—speaks to the problem and solves the matter.
3. When it comes to following a specific plan, **a word of wisdom** can provide invaluable guidance and specific instructions on how to respond.

"Frustration is the enemy of the prophetic."—Graham Cooke

While operating in the Seer flow: In order to perform this action properly, it is crucial that you start it from a state of rest and smoothly transition into a higher momentum. Being at rest when prophesying is important.

Know how you receive your prophetic insight or foresight.

o Without proper training, the level of prophetic ability is characterized by a lack of sharpness and precision.
o Through training, the level of prophetic ability can be honed to become precise, acute, and concise.
o Rather than being a loner with the duty of constantly checking on the kings or priests, the New Testament prophet takes on the role of a catalyst within the church.

But if all prophesy, and there come in one that believeth not, or one unlearned, he is convinced of all, he is judged of all: And thus are the secrets of his heart made manifest; and so falling down on his face he will worship God, and report that God is in you of a truth. —1 Corinthians 14:24

- Reflections, Reviews, Questions

73. Why is it important for a newbie to stick to the basics while prophesying until taking more risks? What are the basics elements to use to help you remain basic?

_____

_____

_____

74. What two things you do makes you more proficient in the prophetic?

_____

_____

_____

75. Show some things discussed about how New Testament prophecies look like today?

_____

_____

_____

76. What is a well-balanced prophetic word may look like?

_____

_____

_____

Notes

_____

_____

_____

_____

_____

_____

_____

_____

_____

Different kinds of prophecies found in the bible[15]

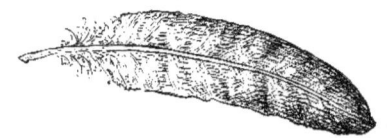

BLESSINGS AND IMPARTATION

PATRIARCHS

By faith Isaac blessed Jacob and Esau concerning things to come. —21 By faith Jacob, when he was a dying, blessed both the sons of Joseph; and worshipped, leaning upon the top of his staff. —22 By faith Joseph, when he died, made mention of the departing of the children of Israel; and gave commandment concerning his bones.— Hebrews 11:20-22

ISAAC'S BLESSING

And it came to pass, that when Isaac was old, and his eyes were dim, so that he could not see, he called Esau his eldest son, and said unto him, My son: and he said unto him, Behold, here am I. —2 And he said, Behold now, I am old, I know not the day of my death: —3 Now therefore take, I pray thee, thy weapons, thy quiver and thy bow, and go out to the field, and take me some venison; —4 And make me savoury meat, such as I love, and bring it to me, that I may eat; that my soul may bless thee before I die. —5 And Rebekah heard when Isaac spake to Esau his son. And Esau went to the field to hunt for venison, and to bring it. —6 And Rebekah spake unto Jacob her son, saying, Behold, I heard thy father speak unto Esau thy brother, saying, —7 Bring me venison, and make me savoury meat, that I may eat, and bless thee before the LORD before my death. —8 Now therefore, my son, obey my voice according to that which I command thee. —9 Go now to the flock, and fetch me from thence two good kids of the goats; and I will make them savoury meat for thy father, such as he loveth: —10 And thou shalt bring it to thy father, that he may eat, and that he may bless thee before his death. —11 And Jacob said to Rebekah his mother, Behold, Esau my brother is a hairy man, and I am a smooth man: —12 My father peradventure will feel me, and I shall seem to him as a deceiver; and I shall bring a curse upon me, and not a blessing. —13 And his mother said unto him, Upon me be thy curse, my son: only obey my voice, and go fetch me them. —14 And he went, and fetched, and brought them to his mother: and his mother made savoury meat, such as his father loved. —15 And Rebekah took goodly raiment of her eldest son Esau, which were with her in the house, and put them upon Jacob her younger son: —16 And she put the skins of the kids of the goats upon his hands, and upon the smooth of his neck: —17 And she gave the savoury meat and the

---

[15] Gordon Lindsay, *Commissioned with Power: An Overview of the Gifts of the Spirit* (Dallas, Tex: Christ for the Nations, 2001).

bread, which she had prepared, into the hand of her son Jacob.   —18 And he came unto his father, and said, My father: and he said, Here am I; who art thou, my son?   —19 And Jacob said unto his father, I am Esau thy firstborn; I have done according as thou badest me: arise, I pray thee, sit and eat of my venison, that thy soul may bless me.   —20 And Isaac said unto his son, How is it that thou hast found it so quickly, my son? And he said, Because the LORD thy God brought it to me.   —21 And Isaac said unto Jacob, Come near, I pray thee, that I may feel thee, my son, whether thou be my very son Esau or not.   —22 And Jacob went near unto Isaac his father; and he felt him, and said, The voice is Jacob's voice, but the hands are the hands of Esau.   —23 And he discerned him not, because his hands were hairy, as his brother Esau's hands: so he blessed him.   —24 And he said, Art thou my very son Esau? And he said, I am.   —25 And he said, Bring it near to me, and I will eat of my son's venison, that my soul may bless thee. And he brought it near to him, and he did eat: and he brought him wine, and he drank.   —26 And his father Isaac said unto him, Come near now, and kiss me, my son.   —27 And he came near, and kissed him: and he smelled the smell of his raiment, and blessed him, and said, See, the smell of my son is as the smell of a field which the LORD hath blessed: —28 Therefore God give thee of the dew of heaven, and the fatness of the earth, and plenty of corn and wine: —29 Let people serve thee, and nations bow down to thee: be lord over thy brethren, and let thy mother's sons bow down to thee: cursed be every one that curseth thee, and blessed be he that blesseth thee.   —30 And it came to pass, as soon as Isaac had made an end of blessing Jacob, and Jacob was yet scarce gone out from the presence of Isaac his father, that Esau his brother came in from his hunting.   —31 And he also had made savoury meat, and brought it unto his father, and said unto his father, Let my father arise, and eat of his son's venison, that thy soul may bless me.   —32 And Isaac his father said unto him, Who art thou? And he said, I am thy son, thy firstborn Esau. —33 And Isaac trembled very exceedingly, and said, Who? where is he that hath taken venison, and brought it me, and I have eaten of all before thou camest, and have blessed him? yea, and he shall be blessed.   —34 And when Esau heard the words of his father, he cried with a great and exceeding bitter cry, and said unto his father, Bless me, even me also, O my father.   —35 And he said, Thy brother came with subtilty, and hath taken away thy blessing.   —36 And he said, Is not he rightly named Jacob? for he hath supplanted me these two times: he took away my birthright; and, behold, now he hath taken away my blessing. And he said, Hast thou not reserved a blessing for me?   —37 And Isaac answered and said unto Esau, Behold, I have made him thy lord, and all his brethren have I given to him for servants; and with corn and wine have I sustained him: and what shall I do now unto thee, my son?   —38 And Esau said unto his father, Hast thou but one blessing, my father? bless me, even me also, O my father. And Esau lifted up his voice, and wept.   —39 And Isaac his father answered and said unto him, Behold, thy dwelling shall be the fatness of the earth, and of the dew of heaven from above;   —40 And by thy sword shalt thou live, and shalt serve thy brother; and it shall come to pass when thou shalt have the dominion, that thou shalt break his yoke from off thy neck.   —41 And Esau hated Jacob because of the blessing wherewith his father blessed him: and Esau said in his heart, The days of mourning for my father are at hand; then will I slay my brother Jacob. —Genesis 27:1-41

ISAAC'S BLESSING FORTHTELLING

Therefore God give thee of the dew of heaven, and the fatness of the earth, and plenty of corn and wine: —29 Let people serve thee, and nations bow down to thee: be lord over thy brethren, and let thy mother's sons bow down to thee: cursed be every one that curseth thee, and blessed be he that blesseth thee. — Genesis 27:28-29

JACOB'S BLESSINGS TO HIS SONS

*And Jacob called unto his sons, and said, **Gather yourselves together, that I may tell you that which shall befall you in the last days**. —2 Gather yourselves together, and hear, ye sons of Jacob; and hearken unto Israel your father. —3 Reuben, thou art my firstborn, my might, and the beginning of my strength, the excellency of dignity, and the excellency of power: —4 Unstable as water, thou shalt not excel; because thou wentest up to thy father's bed; then defiledst thou it: he went up to my couch. —5 Simeon and Levi are brethren; instruments of cruelty are in their habitations. —6 O my soul, come not thou into their secret; unto their assembly, mine honour, be not thou united: for in their anger they slew a man, and in their selfwill they digged down a wall. —7 Cursed be their anger, for it was fierce; and their wrath, for it was cruel: I will divide them in Jacob, and scatter them in Israel. —8 **Judah, thou art he whom thy brethren shall praise: thy hand shall be in the neck of thine enemies; thy father's children shall bow down before thee. —9 Judah is a lion's whelp: from the prey, my son, thou art gone up: he stooped down, he couched as a lion, and as an old lion; who shall rouse him up? —10 The sceptre shall not depart from Judah, nor a lawgiver from between his feet, until Shiloh come; and unto him shall the gathering of the people be. —11 Binding his foal unto the vine, and his ass's colt unto the choice vine; he washed his garments in wine, and his clothes in the blood of grapes: —12 His eyes shall be red with wine, and his teeth white with milk.** —13 Zebulun shall dwell at the haven of the sea; and he shall be for an haven of ships; and his border shall be unto Zidon. —14 Issachar is a strong ass couching down between two burdens: —15 And he saw that rest was good, and the land that it was pleasant; and bowed his shoulder to bear, and became a servant unto tribute. —16 Dan shall judge his people, as one of the tribes of Israel. —17 Dan shall be a serpent by the way, an adder in the path, that biteth the horse heels, so that his rider shall fall backward. —18 I have waited for thy salvation, O LORD. —19 Gad, a troop shall overcome him: but he shall overcome at the last. —20 Out of Asher his bread shall be fat, and he shall yield royal dainties. —21 Naphtali is a hind let loose: he giveth goodly words. —22 Joseph is a fruitful bough, even a fruitful bough by a well; whose branches run over the wall: —23 The archers have sorely grieved him, and shot at him, and hated him: —24 But his bow abode in strength, and the arms of his hands were made strong by the hands of the mighty God of Jacob; (from thence is the shepherd, the stone of Israel:) —25 Even by the God of thy father, who shall help thee; and by the Almighty, who shall bless thee with blessings of heaven above, blessings of the deep that lieth under, blessings of the breasts, and of the womb: —26 The blessings of thy father have prevailed above the blessings of my progenitors unto the utmost bound of the everlasting hills: they shall be on the head of Joseph, and on the crown of the head of him that was separate from his brethren. —27 Benjamin shall ravin as a wolf: in the morning he shall devour the prey, and at night he shall divide the spoil. —28 All these are the twelve tribes of Israel: and this is it that their father spake unto them, and blessed them; every one according to his blessing he blessed them. —29 And he charged them, and said unto them, I am to be gathered unto my people: bury me with my fathers in the cave that is in the field of Ephron the Hittite, —30 In the cave that is in the field of Machpelah, which is before Mamre, in the land of Canaan, which Abraham bought with the field of Ephron the Hittite for a possession of a burying* place. —31 There they buried Abraham and Sarah his wife; there they buried Isaac and Rebekah his wife; and there I buried Leah. —32 The purchase of the field and of the cave that is therein was from the children of Heth. —33 And when Jacob had made an end of commanding his sons, he gathered up his feet into the bed, and yielded up the ghost, and was gathered unto his people.—Genesis 49:1-33

These patriarchal prophecies in the form of impartation blessings from the fathers to the sons was made by faith.

PROPHETIC SONGS IN THE BIBLE

And they sing the song of Moses the servant of God, and the song of the Lamb, saying, Great and marvellous are thy works, Lord God Almighty; just and true are thy ways, thou King of saints. —4 Who shall not fear thee, O Lord, and glorify thy name? for thou only art holy: for all nations shall come and worship before thee; for thy judgments are made manifest.— Revelation 15:3-4

O come, let us sing unto the LORD: let us make a joyful noise to the rock of our salvation. —2 Let us come before his presence with thanksgiving, and make a joyful noise unto him with psalms. —3 For the LORD is a great God, and a great King above all gods. —4 In his hand are the deep places of the earth: the strength of the hills is his also. —5 The sea is his, and he made it: and his hands formed the dry land. —6 O come, let us worship and bow down: let us kneel before the LORD our maker. —7 For he is our God; and we are the people of his pasture, and the sheep of his hand. To day if ye will hear his voice, — Psalms 95:1-7

O sing unto the LORD a new song: sing unto the LORD, all the earth. —Psalms 96:1

Sing unto the LORD a new song, and his praise from the end of the earth, ye that go down to the sea, and all that is therein; the isles, and the inhabitants thereof. —Isaiah 42:10

I will sing a new song unto thee, O God: upon a psaltery and an instrument of ten strings will I sing praises unto thee. —Psalms 144:9

Then sang Moses and the children of Israel this song unto the LORD, and spake, saying, I will sing unto the LORD, for he hath triumphed gloriously: the horse and his rider hath he thrown into the sea. The LORD is my strength and song, and he is become my salvation: he is my God, and I will prepare him an habitation; my father's God, and I will exalt him. The LORD is a man of war: the LORD is his name. Pharaoh's chariots and his host hath he cast into the sea: his chosen captains also are drowned in the Red sea. The depths have covered them: they sank into the bottom as a stone. Thy right hand, O LORD, is become glorious in power: thy right hand, O LORD, hath dashed in pieces the enemy. And in the greatness of thine excellency thou hast overthrown them that rose up against thee: thou sentest forth thy wrath, which consumed them as stubble. And with the blast of thy nostrils the waters were gathered together, the floods stood upright as an heap, and the depths were congealed in the heart of the sea. The enemy said, I will pursue, I will overtake, I will divide the spoil; my lust shall be satisfied upon them; I will draw my sword, my hand shall destroy them. Thou didst blow with thy wind, the sea covered them: they sank as lead in the mighty waters. Who is like unto thee, O LORD, among the gods? who is like thee, glorious in holiness, fearful in praises, doing wonders? Thou stretchedst out thy right hand, the earth swallowed them. Thou in thy mercy hast led forth the people which thou hast redeemed: thou hast guided them in thy strength unto thy holy habitation. The people shall hear, and be afraid: sorrow shall take hold on the inhabitants of Palestina. Then the dukes of Edom shall be amazed; the mighty men of Moab, trembling shall take hold upon them; all the inhabitants of Canaan shall melt away. Fear and dread shall fall upon them; by the greatness of thine arm they shall be as still as a stone; till thy people pass over, O LORD, till the people pass over, which thou hast purchased. Thou shalt bring them in, and plant them in the mountain of thine inheritance, in the place, O LORD, which thou hast made for thee to dwell in, in the Sanctuary, O Lord, which thy hands have established. The LORD shall reign for ever and ever. For the horse of Pharaoh went in with his chariots and with his horsemen into the sea, and the LORD brought again the waters of the sea upon them; but the children of Israel went on dry land in the midst of the sea. And Miriam the prophetess, the sister of Aaron, took a timbrel in her hand; and all the women went out after her with timbrels and with dances. And Miriam answered them, Sing ye to the LORD, for he hath triumphed gloriously; the horse and his rider hath he thrown into the sea. So Moses brought Israel from the Red sea, and they went out into the wilderness of Shur; and they went three days in the wilderness, and found no water. And when they came to Marah, they could not drink of the waters of Marah, for they were bitter: therefore the name of it was called Marah. And the people murmured against Moses, saying, What shall we drink? And he cried unto the LORD; and the LORD shewed him a tree, which when he had cast into the waters, the waters were made sweet: there he made for them a statute and an ordinance, and there he proved them, And said, If thou wilt diligently hearken to the voice of the LORD thy God, and wilt do that which is right in his sight, and wilt give ear to his commandments, and keep all his statutes, I will put none of these diseases upon thee, which I have brought upon the Egyptians: for I am the LORD that healeth thee. And they came to Elim, where were twelve wells of water, and threescore and ten palm trees: and they encamped there by the waters. —Exodus 15:1-27

Then sang Deborah and Barak the son of Abinoam on that day, saying, Praise ye the LORD for the avenging of Israel, when the people willingly offered themselves. Hear, O ye kings; give ear, O ye princes; I, even I, will sing unto the LORD; I will sing praise to the LORD God of Israel. LORD, when thou wentest out of Seir, when thou marchedst out of the field of Edom, the earth trembled, and the heavens dropped, the clouds also dropped water. The mountains melted from before the LORD, even that Sinai from before the LORD God of Israel. In the days of Shamgar the son of Anath, in the days of Jael, the highways were unoccupied, and the travellers walked through byways. The inhabitants of the villages ceased, they ceased in Israel, until that I Deborah arose, that I arose a mother in Israel. They chose new gods; then was war in the gates: was there a shield or spear seen among forty thousand in Israel? My heart is toward the governors of Israel, that offered themselves willingly among the people. Bless ye the LORD. Speak, ye that ride on white asses, ye that sit in judgment, and walk by the way. They that are delivered from the noise of archers in the places of drawing water, there shall they rehearse the righteous acts of the LORD, even the righteous acts toward the inhabitants of his villages in Israel: then shall the people of the LORD go down to the gates. Awake, awake, Deborah: awake, awake, utter a song: arise, Barak, and lead thy captivity captive, thou son of Abinoam. Then he made him that remaineth have dominion over the nobles among the people: the LORD made me have dominion over the mighty. —Judges 5:1-13

Sing, O daughter of Zion; shout, O Israel; be glad and rejoice with all the heart, O daughter of Jerusalem. The LORD hath taken away thy judgments, he hath cast out thine enemy: the king of Israel, even the LORD, is in the midst of thee: thou shalt not see evil any more. In that day it shall be said to Jerusalem, Fear thou not: and to Zion, Let not thine hands be slack. The LORD thy God in the midst of thee is mighty;

he will save, he will rejoice over thee with joy; he will rest in his love, he will joy over thee with singing. I will gather them that are sorrowful for the solemn assembly, who are of thee, to whom the reproach of it was a burden. Behold, at that time I will undo all that afflict thee: and I will save her that halteth, and gather her that was driven out; and I will get them praise and fame in every land where they have been put to shame. At that time will I bring you again, even in the time that I gather you: for I will make you a name and a praise among all people of the earth, when I turn back your captivity before your eyes, saith the LORD. —Zephaniah 3:14-20

CHURCH ARCHITECTURAL PROPHECIES (EDIFICATION)

---

*He that speaketh in an unknown tongue edifieth himself; but **he that prophesieth edifieth the church**. —1 Corinthians 14:4*

---

*And Simon Peter answered and said, Thou art the Christ, the Son of the living God. And Jesus answered and said unto him, Blessed art thou, Simon Barjona: for flesh and blood hath not **revealed** it unto thee, but my **Father which is in heaven.** And I say also unto thee, That thou art Peter, and upon **this rock I will build my church**; and the gates of hell shall not prevail against it. And **I will give unto thee the keys of the kingdom of heaven:** and whatsoever thou <u>shalt bind on earth shall be bound in heaven:</u> and whatsoever <u>thou shalt loose on earth shall be loosed in heaven.</u>*
—Matthew 16:16-19

PROPHECY ABOUT THE MESSIAH

Who hath believed our report? and to whom is the arm of the LORD revealed? —2 For he shall grow up before him as a tender plant, and as a root out of a dry ground: he hath no form nor comeliness; and when we shall see him, there is no beauty that we should desire him. —3 He is despised and rejected of men; a man of sorrows, and acquainted with grief: and we hid as it were our faces from him; he was despised, and we esteemed him not. —4 Surely he hath borne our griefs, and carried our sorrows: yet we did esteem him stricken, smitten of God, and afflicted. —5 But he was wounded for our transgressions, he was bruised for our iniquities: the chastisement of our peace was upon him; and with his stripes we are healed. —6 All we like sheep have gone astray; we have turned every one to his own way; and the LORD hath laid on him the iniquity of us all. —7 He was oppressed, and he was afflicted, yet he opened not his mouth: he is brought as a lamb to the slaughter, and as a sheep before her shearers is dumb, so he openeth not his mouth. —8 He was taken from prison and from judgment: and who shall declare his generation? for he was cut off out of the land of the living: for the transgression of my people was he stricken. —9 And he made his grave with the wicked, and with the rich in his death; because he had done no violence, neither was any deceit in his mouth. —10 Yet it pleased the LORD to bruise him; he hath put him to grief: when thou shalt make his soul an offering for sin, he shall see his seed, he shall prolong his days, and the pleasure of the LORD shall prosper in his hand. —11 He shall see of the travail of his soul, and shall be satisfied: by his knowledge shall my righteous servant justify many; for he shall bear their iniquities. —12 Therefore will I divide him a portion with the great, and he shall divide the spoil with the strong; because he hath poured out his soul unto death: and he was numbered with the transgressors; and he bare the sin of many, and made intercession for the transgressors.— Isaiah 53:1-12

Messianic Psalms: Establishment of the Kingdom of God

Why do the heathen rage, and the people imagine a vain thing? —2 The kings of the earth set themselves, and the rulers take counsel together, against the LORD, and against his anointed, saying, —3 Let us break their bands asunder, and cast away their cords from us. —4 He that sitteth in the heavens shall laugh: the Lord shall have them in derision. —5 Then shall he speak unto them in his wrath, and vex them in his sore displeasure. —6 Yet have I set my king upon my holy hill of Zion. —7 I will declare the decree: the LORD hath said unto me, Thou art my Son; this day have I begotten thee. —8 Ask of me, and I shall give thee the heathen for thine inheritance, and the uttermost parts of the earth for thy possession. —9 Thou shalt break them with a rod of iron; thou shalt dash them in pieces like a potter's vessel. —10 Be wise now therefore, O ye kings: be instructed, ye judges of the earth. —11 Serve the LORD with fear, and rejoice with trembling. —12 Kiss the Son, lest he be angry, and ye perish from the way, when his wrath is kindled but a little. Blessed are all they that put their trust in him. — Psalms 2:1-12

Christ's Death and Descent into Hades

Michtam of David. Preserve me, O God: for in thee do I put my trust. —2 O my soul, thou hast said unto the LORD, Thou art my Lord: my goodness extendeth not to thee; —3 But to the saints that are in the earth, and to the excellent, in whom is all my delight. —4 Their sorrows shall be multiplied that hasten after another god: their drink offerings of blood will I not offer, nor take up their names into my lips. —5 The LORD is the portion of mine inheritance and of my cup: thou maintainest my lot. —6 The lines are fallen unto me in pleasant places; yea, I have a goodly heritage. —7 I will bless the LORD, who hath given me counsel: my reins also instruct me in the night seasons. —8 I have set the LORD always before me: because he is at my right hand, I shall not be moved. —9 Therefore my heart is glad, and my glory rejoiceth: my flesh also shall rest in hope. —10 For thou wilt not leave my soul in hell; neither wilt thou suffer thine Holy One to see corruption. —11 Thou wilt shew me the path of life: in thy presence is fulness of joy; at thy right hand there are pleasures for evermore.— Psalms 16:1-11

The Crucifixion

To the chief Musician upon Aijeleth Shahar, A Psalm of David.

<u>My God, my God, why hast thou forsaken me?</u> why art thou so far from helping me, and from the words of my roaring? —2 O my God, I cry in the daytime, but thou hearest not; and in the night season, and am not silent. —3 But thou art holy, O thou that inhabitest the praises of Israel. —4 Our fathers trusted in thee: they trusted, and thou didst deliver them. —5 They cried unto thee, and were delivered: they trusted in thee, and were not confounded. —6 But I am a worm, and no man; a reproach of men, and despised of the people. —7 All they that see me laugh me to scorn: they shoot out the lip, they shake

the head, saying, —8 He trusted on the LORD that he would deliver him: let him deliver him, seeing he delighted in him. —9 But thou art he that took me out of the womb: thou didst make me hope when I was upon my mother's breasts. —10 I was cast upon thee from the womb: thou art my God from my mother's belly. —11 Be not far from me; for trouble is near; for there is none to help. —12 *Many bulls have compassed me: strong bulls of Bashan have beset me round.* —13 *They gaped upon me with their mouths, as a ravening and a roaring lion.* —14 *I am poured out like water, and all my bones are out of joint: my heart is like wax; it is melted in the midst of my bowels.* —15 *My strength is dried up like a potsherd; and my tongue cleaveth to my jaws; and thou hast brought me into the dust of death.* —16 *For dogs have compassed me: the assembly of the wicked have inclosed me: they pierced my hands and my feet.* —17 *I may tell all my bones: they look and stare upon me.* —18 *They part my garments among them, and cast lots upon my vesture.* —19 *But be not thou far from me, O LORD: O my strength, haste thee to help me.* —Psalms 22:1-19

THE GOOD SHEPHERD (DESCENT)

A Psalm of David.

A Psalm of David. The LORD is my shepherd; I shall not want. —2 He maketh me to lie down in green pastures: he leadeth me beside the still waters. —3 He restoreth my soul: he leadeth me in the paths of righteousness for his name's sake. —4 Yea, though I walk through the valley of the shadow of death, I will fear no evil: for thou art with me; thy rod and thy staff they comfort me. —5 Thou preparest a table before me in the presence of mine enemies: thou anointest my head with oil; my cup runneth over. —6 Surely goodness and mercy shall follow me all the days of my life: and I will dwell in the house of the LORD for ever. — Psalms 23:1-6

ASCENSION

A Psalm of David.

The earth is the LORD'S, and the fulness thereof; the world, and they that dwell therein. —2 For he hath founded it upon the seas, and established it upon the floods. —3 *Who shall ascend into the hill of the LORD?* or who shall stand in his holy place? —4 *He that hath clean hands, and a pure heart;* who hath not lifted up his soul unto vanity, nor sworn deceitfully. —5 He shall receive the blessing from the LORD, and righteousness from the God of his salvation. —6 This is the generation of them that seek him, that seek thy face, O Jacob. Selah. —7 Lift up your heads, O ye gates; and be ye lift up, ye everlasting doors; and the King of glory shall come in. —8 Who is this King of glory? The LORD strong and mighty, the LORD mighty in battle. —9 Lift up your heads, O ye gates; even lift them up, ye everlasting doors; and the King of glory shall come in. —10 *Who is this King of glory? The LORD of hosts, he is the King of glory.* Selah.— Psalms 24:1-10

MESSIANIC KINGDOM

> *For God will save Zion, and will build the cities of Judah: that they may dwell there, and have it in possession. —Psalms 69:35*

THE BRIDEGROOM CALLING HIS BRIDE

To the Chief Musician. Set to "The Lilies." A Contemplation of the Sons of Korah. A Song of Love.

> *My heart is inditing a good matter: I speak of the things which I have made touching the king: my tongue is the pen of a ready writer. —2 Thou art fairer than the children of men: grace is poured into thy lips: therefore God hath blessed thee for ever. —3 Gird thy sword upon thy thigh, O most mighty, with thy glory and thy majesty. —4 And in thy majesty ride prosperously because of truth and meekness and righteousness; and thy right hand shall teach thee terrible things. —5 Thine arrows are sharp in the heart of the king's enemies; whereby the people fall under thee. —6 Thy throne, O God, is for ever and ever: the sceptre of thy kingdom is a right sceptre. —7 Thou lovest righteousness, and hatest wickedness: therefore God, thy God, hath anointed thee with the oil of gladness above thy fellows. —8 All thy garments smell of myrrh, and aloes, and cassia, out of the ivory palaces, whereby they have made thee glad. —9 Kings' daughters were among thy honourable women: upon thy right hand did stand the queen in gold of Ophir. —10 Hearken, O daughter, and consider, and incline thine ear; forget also thine own people, and thy father's house; —11 So shall the king greatly desire thy beauty: for he is thy Lord; and worship thou him. —12 And the daughter of Tyre shall be there with a gift; even the rich among the people shall intreat thy favour. —13 The king's daughter is all glorious within: her clothing is of wrought gold. —14 She shall be brought unto the king in raiment of needlework: the virgins her companions that follow her shall be brought unto thee. —15 With gladness and rejoicing shall they be brought: they shall enter into the king's palace. —16 Instead of thy fathers shall be thy children, whom thou mayest make princes in all the earth. —17 I will make thy name to be remembered in all generations: therefore shall the people praise thee for ever and ever.— Psalms 45:1-17*

PROPHESY TOWARD THE UNBELIEVERS

> *But if all prophesy, and there come in <u>one that believeth</u> not, or one unlearned, he is convinced of all, he is judged of all: —25 And thus are **<u>the secrets of his heart made manifest</u>**; and <u>so falling down on his face he will worship God</u>, and <u>report that God is in you of a truth.</u> — 1 Corinthians 14:24-25*

This is where we see the third part of the definition of prophecy being defined in the bible. The part which we said the prophetic not only deals with forthtelling and foretelling, but also the revealing of mysteries and knowledge, whether in this case personal or congregational, or national. The Word of Knowledge element of the prophetic is a power tool of diagnosis or reading mail. It reveals the deep secret of a men's hearts.

*And Samuel answered Saul, and said, <u>I am the seer</u>; go up before me unto the high place; for ye shall eat with me to day, and tomorrow **I will let thee go, and will tell thee all that is in thine heart.** And as for thine asses that were lost three days ago, set not thy mind on them; for they are found. And on whom is all the desire of Israel? Is it not on thee, and on all thy father's house? —1 Samuel 9:19-20*

In the passage above we see the operation of the word of knowledge when Samuel the seer read the heart of Saul. He also told Saul about the donkeys he lost were found and not to worry about them and they have been found. He also prophesied about his future position as king.

CONDITIONAL PROPHECIES

WICKED TURNING TO GOD AND GOOD TURNING AWAY FROM GOD

*When I shall say to the righteous, that he shall surely live; if he trust to his own righteousness, and commit iniquity, all his righteousnesses shall not be remembered; but for his iniquity that he hath committed, he shall die for it. —14 Again, when I say unto the wicked, **Thou shalt surely die; if he turn from his sin, and do that which is lawful and right;** —15 **If the wicked restore the pledge, give again that he had robbed, walk in the statutes of life, without committing iniquity; he shall surely live, he shall not die.** —16 None of his sins that he hath committed shall be mentioned unto him: he hath done that which is lawful and right; he shall surely live. —Ezekiel 33:13-16*

UNCONDITIONAL PROPHECIES

Most of the prophecies found in the bible are unconditional with some exceptions. The prophecies about the messiah life, death, burial, and resurrection where definitively unconditional and all were fulfilled.

Who hath believed our report? and to whom is the arm of the LORD revealed? —2 For he shall grow up before him as a tender plant, and as a root out of a dry ground: he hath no form nor comeliness; and when we shall see him, there is no beauty that we should desire him. —3 He is despised and rejected of men; a man of sorrows, and acquainted with grief: and we hid as it were our faces from him; he was despised, and we esteemed him not. —4 Surely he hath borne our griefs, and carried our sorrows: yet we did esteem him stricken, smitten of God, and afflicted. —5 But he was wounded for our transgressions, he was bruised for our iniquities: the chastisement of our peace was upon him; and with his stripes we are healed. —6 All we like sheep have gone astray; we have turned every one to his own way; and the LORD hath laid on him the iniquity of us all. —7 He was oppressed, and he was afflicted, yet he opened not his mouth: he is brought as a lamb to the slaughter, and as a sheep before her shearers is dumb, so he openeth not his mouth. —8 He was taken from prison and from judgment: and who shall declare his generation? for he was cut off out of the land of the living: for the transgression of my people was he stricken. —9 And he made his grave with the wicked, and with the rich in his death; because he had done no violence, neither was any deceit in his mouth. —10 Yet it pleased the LORD to bruise him; he hath put him to grief: when thou shalt make his soul an offering for sin, he shall see his seed, he shall prolong his days, and the pleasure of the LORD shall prosper in his hand. —11 He shall see of the travail of his soul, and shall be satisfied: by his knowledge shall my righteous servant justify many; for he shall bear their iniquities. —12 Therefore will I divide him a portion with the great, and he shall divide the spoil with the strong; because he hath poured out his soul unto death: and he was numbered with the transgressors; and he bare the sin of many, and made intercession for the transgressors.— Isaiah 53:1-12

END-TIME PROPHECIES OR APOCALYPTIC PROPHECIES

Blessed is he that readeth, and they that hear the words of this prophecy, and keep those things which are written therein: for the time is at hand. —Revelation 1:3

HEZEKIAH'S ILLNESS AND RECOVERY

*In those days was Hezekiah sick unto death. And the prophet Isaiah the son of Amoz came to him, and said unto him, **Thus saith the LORD, Set thine house in order; for thou shalt die, and not live.** —2 Then he turned his face to the wall, and prayed unto the LORD, saying, —3 I beseech thee, O LORD, remember now how I have walked before thee in truth and with a perfect heart, and have done that which is good in thy sight. And Hezekiah wept sore. —4 And it came to pass, afore Isaiah was gone out into the middle court, that the word of the LORD came to him, saying, —5 Turn again, and tell Hezekiah the captain of my people, **Thus saith the LORD, the God of David thy father, I have heard thy prayer, I have seen thy tears: behold, I will heal thee: on the third day thou shalt go up unto the house of the LORD. —6 And I will add unto thy days fifteen years; and I will deliver thee and this city out of the hand of the king of Assyria; and I will defend this city for mine own sake, and for my servant David's sake.** —7 And Isaiah said, Take a lump of figs. And they took and laid it on the boil, and he recovered. —8 And Hezekiah said unto Isaiah, What shall be the sign that the LORD will heal me, and that I shall go up into the house of the LORD the third day? —9 And Isaiah said, This sign shalt thou have of the LORD, that the LORD will do the thing that he hath spoken: shall the shadow go forward ten degrees, or go back ten degrees? —10 And Hezekiah answered, It is a light thing for the shadow to go down ten degrees: nay, but let the shadow return backward ten degrees. —11 And Isaiah the prophet cried unto the LORD: and he brought the shadow ten degrees backward, by which it had gone down in the dial of Ahaz. — 2 Kings 20:1-11*

JONAH AND NINEVEH'S DESTRUCTION

*And the word of the LORD came unto Jonah the second time, saying, —2 Arise, go unto Nineveh, that great city, and preach unto it the preaching that I bid thee. —3 So Jonah arose, and went unto Nineveh, according to the word of the LORD. Now Nineveh was an exceeding great city of three days' journey. —4 And Jonah began to enter into the city a day's journey, and he cried, and said, <u>Yet forty days, and Nineveh shall be overthrown.</u> —5 <u>So the people of Nineveh believed God, and proclaimed a fast, and put on sackcloth, from the greatest of them even to the least of them.</u> —6 For word came unto the king of Nineveh, and he arose from his throne, and he laid his robe from him, and covered him with sackcloth, and sat in ashes. —7 And he caused it to be proclaimed and published through Nineveh by the decree of the king and his nobles, saying, Let neither man nor beast, herd nor flock, taste any thing: let them not feed, nor drink water: —8 But let man and beast be covered with sackcloth, and cry mightily unto God: yea, let them turn every one from his evil way, and from the violence that is in their hands. —9 <u>Who can tell if God will turn and repent, and turn away from his fierce anger, that we perish not?</u> —10 And **God saw their works, that they turned from their evil way; and God repented of the evil, that he had said that he would do unto them; and he did it not.** — Jonah 3:1-10*

THE PROPHECIES MADE BY JESUS

Woe unto thee, Chorazin! woe unto thee, Bethsaida! for if the mighty works, which were done in you, had been done in Tyre and Sidon, they would have repented long ago in sackcloth and ashes. —22 But I say unto you, It shall be more tolerable for Tyre and Sidon at the day of judgment, than for you. —23 And thou, Capernaum, which art exalted unto heaven, shalt be brought down to hell: for if the mighty works, which have been done in thee, had been done in Sodom, it would have remained until this day. —24 But I say unto you, That it shall be more tolerable for the land of Sodom in the day of judgment, than for thee. —Matthew 11:21-24

When evening had come, He sat down with the twelve. Now as they were eating, He said, "Assuredly, I say to you, one of you will betray Me." —Matthew 26:20-21

And when they had sung a hymn, they went out to the Mount of Olives. —31 Then Jesus said to them, "All of you will be made to stumble because of Me this night, for it is written: 'I WILL STRIKE THE SHEPHERD, AND THE SHEEP OF THE FLOCK WILL BE SCATTERED.' —32 But after I have been raised, I will go before you to Galilee." —33 Peter answered and said to Him, "Even if all are made to stumble because of You, I will never be made to stumble." —34 Jesus said to him, "Assuredly, I say to you that this night, before the rooster crows, you will deny Me three times." —35 Peter said to Him, "Even if I have to die with You, I will not deny You!" And so said all the disciples. - Matthew 26:30-35

Now Jesus, going up to Jerusalem, took the twelve disciples aside on the road and said to them, —18 "Behold, we are going up to Jerusalem, and the Son of Man will be betrayed to the chief priests and to the scribes; and they will condemn Him to death, —19 and deliver Him to the Gentiles to mock and to scourge and to crucify. And the third day He will rise again." —20 Then the mother of Zebedee's sons came to Him with her sons, kneeling down and asking something from Him. — Matthew 20:17-20

Then Jesus went out and departed from the temple, and His disciples came up to show Him the buildings of the temple. And Jesus said to them, "Do you not see all these things? Assuredly, I say to you, not one stone shall be left here upon another, that shall not be thrown down." —Matthew 24:1-2

JESUS WEEPS OVER THE DESTRUCTION OF JERUSALEM AND THE REASONS FOR ITS IMPENDING DESTRUCTION.

Now as He drew near, He saw the city and wept over it, —42 saying, "If you had known, even you, especially in this your day, the things that make for your peace! But now they are hidden from your eyes. —43 For days will come upon you when your enemies will build an embankment around you, surround you and close you in on every side, —44 and level you, and your children within you, to the ground; and they will not leave in you one stone upon another, because you did not know the time of your visitation."— Luke 19:41-44 NKJV

JESUS FORETELLS DESTRUCTION OF JERUSALEM

Now as He drew near, He saw the city and wept over it, —42 saying, "If you had known, even you, especially in this your day, the things that make for your peace! But now they are hidden from your eyes. —43 For days will come upon you when your enemies will build an embankment around you, surround you and close you in on every side, —44 and level you, and your children within you, to the ground; and they will not leave in you one stone upon another, because you did not know the time of your visitation."— Luke 21:20-24

THE HIGH PRIEST CAIAPHAS PROPHECY ABOUT JESUS

And one of them, Caiaphas, being high priest that year, said to them, "You know nothing at all, —50 nor do you consider that it is expedient for us that one man should die for the people, and not that the whole nation should perish." —51 Now this he did not say on his own authority; but being high priest that year he prophesied that Jesus would die for the nation, —52 and not for that nation only, but also that He would gather together in one the children of God who were scattered abroad. —53 Then, from that day on, they plotted to put Him to death. —54 Therefore Jesus no longer walked openly among the Jews, but went from there into the country near the wilderness, to a city called Ephraim, and there remained with His disciples. —55 And the Passover of the Jews was near, and many went from the country up to Jerusalem before the Passover, to purify themselves. —56 Then they sought Jesus, and spoke among themselves as they stood in the temple, "What do you think—that He will not come to the feast?" —57 Now both the chief priests and the Pharisees had given a command, that if anyone knew where He was, he should report it, that they might seize Him. —John 11:49-57

ELIJAH'S FIRST WORD

And Elijah the Tishbite, of the inhabitants of Gilead, said to Ahab, "<u>As the LORD God of Israel lives, before whom I stand,</u> there shall not be dew nor rain these years, except at my word." —2 Then the word of the LORD came to him, saying, —3 "Get away from here and turn eastward, and hide by the Brook Cherith, which flows into the Jordan. —4 And it will be that you shall drink from the brook, and I have commanded the ravens to feed you there."— 1 Kings 17:1-4

THE LORD DID NOT ALLOW NONE OF SAMUEL'S WORD FALL TO THE GROUND

So Samuel grew, and <u>the LORD was with him</u> and let none of his words fall to the ground. —20 And all Israel from Dan to Beersheba knew that Samuel had been established as a prophet of the LORD. —21 Then the LORD appeared again in Shiloh. For the LORD revealed Himself to Samuel in Shiloh by the word of the LORD.— 1 Samuel 3:19-21

- Reflections, Reviews, Questions

77. Find one of the listed prophetic words found in the bible and make a commentary about it below:

_____

_____

78. If a prophetic word is conditional does the receiver have to be in obedience to God and the Word of the Lord for the prophetic word to be fulfilled?

_____

_____

79. Explain the difference between conditional and unconditional prophecies.

_____

_____

80. Give the best biblical examples of an unconditional prophecy and a conditional prophecy.

_____

_____

81. Do you believe that most personal prophecies are predominantly conditional or unconditional?

_____

_____

82. Do you have any idea as to why the Lord didn't allow Samuel's word to not fall to the ground?

_____

_____

Notes

_____

_____

_____

_____

_____

Thus says the Lord

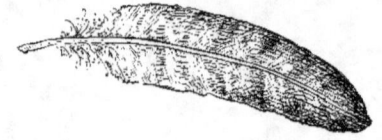

RECOMMEND WORDS TO USE AS PREFIX AND POSTFIX INSTEAD OF "THUS SAYS THE LORD"

In the previous generation, there has been a significant amount of abuse in the prophetic realm, primarily stemming from individuals imposing their own impressions as divine messages. We prophesy in part. Impressions and dark sayings are characterized by their subtle nature, making them prone to misinterpretation. In addition to the fact that the majority of personal prophecies are conditional, it is crucial to utilize appropriate language in order to effectively communicate our understanding of God's message. In the realm of Glory, there are specific moments when you receive a distinct and certain message from the Lord, and it is your responsibility to declare it precisely as you heard it. In cases like this, it is advisable to use words like "Thus says the Lord" with caution. In the schools of the prophetic, our main focus is on developing the abilities to effectively encourage, comfort, edify, and exhort people, with the ultimate goal of spending extensive hours in the prophetic realm. By consistently operating in the prophetic realm, we gradually build faith and certainty in the messages we receive. This, in turn, provides us with a reliable track record and the confidence needed to take bolder risks with the Lord's guidance. Receiving words of knowledge entails the utilization of multiple mechanics to access supernatural information. The words of knowledge, when put simply, provide us with a strong foundation of faith that allows us to bounce higher into the future prophetic words. Future prophetic words cannot be validated until they have been fulfilled. Although there may be those who affirm the testimony of another witness who has foretold the same events, our complete recognition of the fulfillment of these prophecies can only be achieved once the prophesied events have materialized. As our prophetic words progressively come to fruition, we witness a strengthening of their foundation and an increasing manifestation of the Lord's favor and assurance, reinforcing our commitment to carefully steward and observe the words we speak. Table 2 on the next page are some alternative expressions that can be employed in place of "Thus Says the Lord" or "The Lord Said." In my belief, the intention is to refrain from imposing anything on the listener and instead, approach with humility, allowing the Lord to validate His own words.

I perceive,	*I discern*
I see,	*I am beholding*
I hear,	*I ascertain that*
I am sensing.	*I am picking up*
What I believe I am seeing is,	*I perceive in my spirit that*
My Insight is	*My impression of the situation...*
I foresee you...	*I have a very strong feeling*
I believe the Father is saying	*The thought that came to*

TABLE 2 RECOMMENDED WORDS TO USE

Suggestions for increasing the Prophetic Anointing (Calibrations).

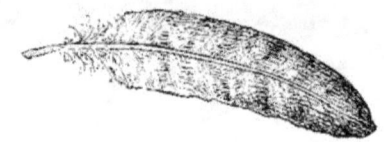

o **Prophetic Culture**

Surround yourself with believers who regularly exercise the prophetic.

o **Spiritual Growth Commitment**

Follow the School of the Holy Spirit 8 Commitment of Being a Spiritual Warrior page 110 of this manual.

o **The Revelation of Jesus**

Incorporate daily reading of Revelation into your routine. Knowing accurate end time eschatology will unlock your prophetic revelatory gift.

o **Pray and Prophesy Daily**

By reason of use.

o **Honor and Sowing**

In addition to the commitment of "giving extravagantly" as outlined in the 8 commitments for being a Spiritual Warrior, it is also important to honor and sow into the ministries of prophetic individuals who have already demonstrated the level of prophetic gifting that you aspire to achieve. Be around them as much as possible and glean on them.

o **Daily calibrations contemplative prayer session in the secret place**

The early bird gets the worm. Waking up in the early morning hours and seeking Him.

O God, thou art my God; early will I seek thee: my soul thirsteth for thee, my flesh longeth for thee... —Psalm 63:1b

With my soul have I desired thee in the night; yea, with my spirit within me will I seek thee early: for when thy judgments are in the earth, the inhabitants of the world will learn righteousness. —Isaiah 26:9

The above list of recommendations limits to the SOP1 course, which specifically caters to the training of the Nabiy flow personal prophecy track. For Seer Flow Calibrations see "School of the Holy Spirit Manual 3b."

Activations, Calibrations & Calisthenics Level 1

Single Word Activation

One word of encouragement and blessing to the person on the hot seat.

The name of the person should be named first then the single word decreed and declared.

These single words are comfort, edify, or exhort. The giver of these single words should write these down on a piece of paper or remember them for later use. Once all the activations are complete, the giver of the one word should change this to a full sentence or phrase.

Through this activation, beginners will come to realize that they have the potential to receive direct communication from the Lord. The most effective approach to teaching reading is to introduce the alphabet first, rather than jumping straight into complete words. In terms of activations, this is the first letter in the Alphabet.

Single Scripture or the entrance of your words gives light

Share a scripture, and it is advised to paraphrase it rather than using exact quotations. You would include the exact verse only in situations where it is advantageous, such as an inheritance scripture word. The Word of God that is released acts as a boomerang effect and doesn't return emptiness, but illuminates the condition of the receiver to the one who release it.

> *So shall My word be that goes forth from My mouth; It shall not return to Me void, But it shall accomplish what I please, And it shall prosper in the thing for which I sent it. —Isaiah 55:11*

> *The entrance of Your words gives light; It gives understanding to the simple. —Psalm 119:130 NKJV*

> *Oh, send out Your light and Your truth! Let them lead me; Let them bring me to Your holy hill And to Your tabernacle. —Psalm 43:3 NKJV*

For the word of God is living and powerful, and sharper than any two-edged sword, piercing even to the division of **soul** *and* **spirit***, and of* **joints and marrow [body]***, and is a discerner of the thoughts and intents of the heart.* —*Hebrew 4:12 NKJV*

It is the Spirit who gives life; the flesh profits nothing. The words that I speak to you **are spirit***, and* **they are life.** —*John 6:63*

SEER ACTIVATION (MENTAL PICTURE) ACTIVATING THE IMAGINATION

In order to enhance your spiritual experience, it is suggested to incorporate the practice of remaining still and focusing on your breath after praying in tongues or uttering the Name of YHVH (pronounced Yod-Hey-Vav-Hey).

Hebrew letters יהוה

Revelation Through (Five Senses) Nabiy & Seer

Learning to use your spiritual senses by receiving words of knowledge through the senses.

God Highlighting (go where God is working)

Words of Knowledge for situations

HOT SEAT ACTIVATIONS[16]

Have one person in a chair in front of the entire audience or classroom and have people line up to prophesy to the individual in the chair.

MYSTERY PERSON ACTIVATION

The instructor will select one person in the group or in the audience and they will instruct the rest of the students to prophesy to this unknown individual is (Child X). This activation encourages trust in the Holy Spirit knowing all things and knowing who this person everyone is prophesying to. The anointing increases in the room much more during this activation. A twist to this activation is to select each person to be their own (Child X) unknown individual (this means they will prophesy to themselves without their own knowledge of it). In order to heighten the prophetic anointing, it is further recommended that the students or participants of this activation make use of the first-person tense.

---

[16] Prophet Lackie, Bill, *Prophetic Activations...Preparing the Gift* (Frontline International), accessed March 22, 2022, https://www.frontlineinternational.com/bill-lackie-audio-teachings/prophetic-activations.

MY TONGUE IS THE PEN OF A READY WRITER. PSALM 45:1C

This activation gives you the thoughts of God for another. Ask the Holy Spirit to write or type through your hand.

JOURNALING THE HEART OF GOD

The goal of this activation is to instruct students on how to discern the Father's heart for others, with a specific emphasis on the Father's love. The first-person tense yields the best results for this activation.

PERCEIVING THE INDIVIDUAL VIA A BIBLICAL NARRATIVE.

Request the Holy Spirit to provide insight into the person's present situation by using a familiar bible story as a means of relating or revealing the situation. This activation work best in first person as God the Father. While it is initially placed at level one, it should be placed at each subsequent level as the complexities continue to increase.

THE FATHER'S RIGHT HAND OF BLESSING (INSPIRED BY PATRICIA KING)

Thumb— The Father's heart and Ministry endeavors

Index Finger— represents the prophetic and the future it holds for the individual.

Middle Finger—Ask the Holy Spirit what is the most important issue in their life at the moment.

Ring Finger—for Relationships and Money related issues

Pinky Finger—delves into the concept of life's equilibrium and how it can intersect with the maintenance of one's health.

Important Note: When discussing specific illnesses, it is crucial to approach the topic with care to avoid mistakenly assigning sicknesses to individuals. One way to do this is by formulating questions instead of making definitive statements.

Activations, Calibrations & Calisthenics Level 2

RIDING ON COATTAILS OR PIGGY BACKING (NABIY FLOW)

The focus of this activation is to develop team synergy through training. As part of the process, we are asking each person to prophesy to the person in the hot seat or chair, building upon the last topic or word that was prophesied by the previous person. If the prophecy made by the first person revolves around finance, it is expected that the subsequent person would either prophesy on the same topic or carry forward from the same last words.

WHO IS THE FATHER HIGHLIGHTING OR MYSTERY PERSON PROPHECY

During this activation, the leader of the team will choose someone from the room. The person chosen by the meeting leader must remain unknown to the public, known only to the Lord and the leader. This activation will result in an increase of the Holy Spirit's anointing in the room, due to the elevated level of trust in the Lord. To help spice things up, when you do this twice, on the second time, the leader should make the blind man or person they are prophesying to themselves. They should also be motivated to consult the Lord regarding the gender of this individual, refraining from disclosing it until they have mastered more of these practices. This will assist individuals in developing confidence in perceiving the Holy Spirit and relying on Him instead of speculating.

SINGING THE HEART OF THE FATHER OR THE BRIDEGROOM KING

Everyone takes time to sing in first person as God the Father would to his daughter or as would Jesus be singing to His Bride. It doesn't matter if you know how to sing or not. The singer will not rely on a previously sung song, but they must create a fresh and brand-new song from the heart. In this activation, singing the Word of the Lord first can bring light and help you enter an additional dimension of worship.

THE PAST, THE PRESENT, AND THE FUTURE

Within this activation, we are employing the word of knowledge to acquire access to diagnosing the individual in the personal prophecy. We then invite the Holy Spirit to disclose both the person's present whereabouts and future trajectory, or to inspire us with a prophetic solution to the diagnosis. We shall begin with the Words of Knowledge, subsequently transitioning to the Words of Prophecy and lastly Words of Wisdom.

SEEING A MENTAL THOUGHT OR IMPRESSION

The majority of our prophetic reception is predominantly derived from mental thoughts and impressions. These pictures appear to be quite subtle until we closely examine the image or the impression. It is necessary for us to intentionally enter the picture to access a greater understanding. Initially, some individuals generate a mental picture, which eventually transitions into a vision or a moving visual representation. The key is to always ask the Holy Spirit questions.

FACE TO FACE

The act of holding hands and facing each other establishes a one-on-one connection. The leader of the group will arrange individuals into pairs for this activation. One individual from the pair will be assigned the role of leader. The activation will be conducted simultaneously by all participants. Here's how it goes: the leader of each group will start by asking the person in front of them. You'll face each other and ask the Holy Spirit for one or two things the Lord wants to bless you with. If you are seeking to push your boundaries and delve into a more intense and profound level of the prophetic anointing, consider choosing individuals who have a closer relational connection to you.

Activations, Calibrations & Calisthenics Level 3

Enter into His gates with thanksgiving, And into His courts with praise. Be thankful to Him, and bless His name. —Psalms 100:4

ENTER HIS GATES WITH THANKSGIVING CALISTHENICS "STRETCH" (NABIY FLOW)

This is one of the best prophetic stretching exercise. To start, offer a prayer of thanks to the Lord for the individual, then proceed to prophesy what you perceive or envision. The duration will be one minute. After completing the iteration for the entire group of four or five personnel, you will reset and commence with a two-minute duration. The leader can choose to either continue incrementing by one minute or exponentially. The objective is to prolong the duration of prophesying sessions by gradually increasing the time intervals, starting from 1 minute and progressing to 2 minutes, 3 minutes, and so forth, all while maintaining a maximum limit of 15 minutes per session. In order to engage in this exercise, it is necessary for every individual, except for the one person who is prophesying, to be praying in tongues. While engaging in prayer in tongues, one should direct the prayer of understanding towards the achievement and prosperity of the person who is prophesying. The main objective of this training is to teach individuals how to excel in the role of a cheerleader, specifically when it comes to supporting and uplifting a person who is prophesying. The prayers will not only act as fuel, but also create a powerful vortex of protection for the person who is prophesying, while at the same time strengthening the faith of each individual involved.

ENTER HIS GATES WITH THANKSGIVING CALISTHENICS "SWITCH"

Once every member of the entire group has completed their prophecies during the aforementioned calisthenics, you may proceed to deliver your prophecy for one minute in the same manner as before. However, this time, after each minute elapses, you must select a different individual and increase the duration to 2 minutes, then 3 minutes, and finally 4 minutes. This will show you how it feels to prophesy to different persons.

Bibliography

Brown, Francis, S. R. Driver, and Charles A. Briggs. *The Brown-Driver-Briggs Hebrew and English Lexicon.* Complete and Unabridged, Fully searchable, with Strong Numbers and Interactive Index edition. Peabody, Mass: Hendrickson Academic, 1994.

"Dictionary by Merriam-Webster: America's Most-Trusted Online Dictionary." Accessed March 26, 2022. https://www.merriam-webster.com/.

Dr. Stuart Pattico. "How to Prophesy and Move in the Prophetic." Accessed March 22, 2022. http://www.stuartpattico.com/2/post/2017/04/how-to-prophesy-and-move-in-the-prophetic.html.

Goll, James W., and Mark Chironna. *The Seer Expanded Edition: The Prophetic Power of Visions, Dreams and Open Heavens.* Expanded edition. Shippensburg, PA: Destiny Image Publishers, 2012.

Lackie, Bill, Prophet. *Prophetic Activations...Preparing the Gift.* Frontline International. Accessed March 22, 2022. https://www.frontlineinternational.com/bill-lackie-audio-teachings/prophetic-activations.

Lindsay, Gordon. *Commissioned with Power: An Overview of the Gifts of the Spirit.* Dallas, Tex: Christ for the Nations, 2001.

Mounce, William D. *Mounce's Complete Expository Dictionary of Old and New Testament Words.* Supersaver ed. edition. Grand Rapids (Mich.): Zondervan Academic, 2006.

Nelson, Thomas. *NKJV, End-of-Verse Reference Bible, Personal Size Large Print, Leathersoft, Black, Red Letter, Comfort Print: Holy Bible, New King James Version.* Large type / Large print edition. Nashville: Thomas Nelson, 2020.

Sandford, John, and Paula Sandford. *The Elijah Task: A Call to Today's Prophets and Intercessors.* Annotated edition. Lake Mary, Fla: Charisma House, 2006.

Selvaraj, Sundar. *Wait As Eagles.* Jesus Ministries, 2015.

Strong, James. *The New Strong's Expanded Exhaustive Concordance of the Bible.* Expanded edition. Thomas Nelson, 2010.

Thayer, Joseph, ed. *Thayer's Greek-English Lexicon of the New Testament: Coded with Strong's Concordance Numbers.* Reissue,Subsequent edition. Massachusetts: Hendrickson Academic, 1995.

8 Commitments for being a Spiritual Warrior

1. **Being a Royal Priest**
    o   **Prioritize** the first commandment: <u>**Love the Lord**</u> with all your heart, soul, and strength. Then, follow the second commandment: <u>**love yourself**</u> first then <u>**love others**</u>.
    o   Priests prioritize <u>safeguarding the Lord's presence</u> in their earthly tabernacle (body and soul) first, then ministering in the heavenly tabernacle (seated in the heavenly places (spirit)).
    o   **Pray Daily** (especially contemplative prayer), Dedicate at least 2 ½ hours a day to prayer.

2. **Cultivate a lifestyle of obedience and worship, rooted in the fear of the Lord.** Make it a daily practice to worship, obey, and read the Word, specifically the Book of Revelation. Fellowship with other believers. *<u>O worship the LORD in the beauty of holiness</u>: fear before him, all the earth. —Psalms 96:9*

3. **Consecrate and be thankful (Fasted Lifestyle).** Regal Priests consecrate themselves in their earthly tabernacle, their bodies, as their daily living sacrifices (per Psalm 24 "ascend") and (per Psalm 15 "dwell") in the heavenly tabernacle. Being Living Stones; Building a Spiritual House; Offer Spiritual Sacrifices of Righteousness; Sacrifices of Trust; Renewing your Mind (1 Peter 2:5, Psalms 4:5).

4. **Pure religion and undefiled before God:** Embrace the responsibility of being a good citizen on Earth by helping the poor, the widows, and the orphans, and lay low (James 1:27).

5. **Honor, Serve and Give extravagantly:** Give to support the kingdom by sowing into those who have paved the way for you.
    o   Give elders double honor. Priest offer gifts and sacrifices to the Lord and the people (*1 Timothy 5:17)*. Support your spiritual leaders with your resources and service.

6. **Make Disciples**: Duplicate yourself and give everything you have to receive more (Matthew 28:19).

7. **Power Evangelism:** He sent them to <u>preach the kingdom of God</u> and <u>to heal the sick</u> (Luke 9:2).
    o   Cleanse the lepers, raise the dead, cast out demons. Prophesy and Win souls.

8. **Lead: Royal Priests Teach & Judge, Sanctify** and act as **ambassadors of His forgiveness**.
    o   Preach the Gospel of the Kingdom by Teaching, Prophesying, Healing the Sick, Raising the dead. Casting out demons. Release SOZO (Greek for Saved, Healed, and Delivered) .

This manual is a supplement to SOP1 course of the School of the Holy Spirit. Consider taking this course by visiting on the SchooloftheProphets.club website or sending an email to admin@schooloftheholyspirit.club. Those who have freely made copies for small groups and church training and would like to give back to the ministry visit SchooloftheHolySpirit.church .

Websites and Social Media

SchooloftheProphets.club

ThierryNakoa.com

SchoolofthePriests.club

ThierryNakoa.club

SchooloftheKings.Club

twitter.com/thierrynakoa

SchooloftheHolySpirit.Club

instagram.com/schooloftheholyspirit.club/

SchooloftheHolySpirit.Church

facebook.com/groups/fireschooloftheholyspirit

Telegram:
https://t.me/+AnpS_QkH5wc0ZDYx

CLUBHOUSE:
https://www.clubhouse.com/c/join/pToMmNIG

ABOUT THE AUTHOR

Thierry's ministry is truly one-of-a-kind, reflecting his strong character and deep desire to introduce Jesus to everyone. Thierry is a Catalyst and an Equipper of the "Bride that is making herself ready." A Pioneer and an Overcomer, a Warrior and a Witness to the Word of God and the Testimony of Jesus Christ. Thierry considers himself to be a brother and saint and companion in the tribulation and kingdom and patience of Jesus Christ. He is also Servant, friend, son of God; A prophet, priest and king in the order of Melchizedek. His disciples hold the belief that he is a revealer of mysteries in the knowledge of Christ. Thierry's influence encourages and sharpens those in his presence, motivating them to reach their full potential and allowing the glory of God to manifest within them. Thierry not only carries the love, but also the joy and fear of the Lord, and generously imparts that divine grace to those around him. The Holy Spirit has sparked a passionate fire in many through his work. Thierry's letters, teachings, and activations, similar to Paul's, have led many to a deeper revelation of the word of God, Holy Spirit, and the supernatural. At the end of the day, Thierry is married to the most beautiful and smartest wife ever, Janette. Janette and Thierry are blessed with a highly intelligent son.

www.ingramcontent.com/pod-product-compliance
Lightning Source LLC
Chambersburg PA
CBHW081336120626
46546CB00011B/3371